BASICS OF BHAGAVAD-GITA

(A thematic study of Bhagavad-gītā)

Based on the teachings of
His Divine Grace
A.C.Bhaktivedanta Swami Prabhupāda
Founder-*Ācārya* of the International Society for Krishna Consciousness

Books by His Divine Grace A. C. Bhaktivedanta Swami Prabhupāda:

Bhagavad-gītā As It Is
Śrīmad-Bhāgavatam (1st to 10th Cantos)
Śrī Caitanya-caritāmṛta (9 vols.)
Kṛṣṇa, The Supreme Personality of Godhead
Teachings of Lord Caitanya
The Nectar of Devotion
The Nectar of Instruction
Śrī Īśopaniṣad
Light of the Bhāgavata
Easy Journey to Other Planets
The Science of Self-Realization
Kṛṣṇa Consciousness: The Topmost Yoga System
Perfect Questions, Perfect Answers
Teachings of Lord Kapila, the Son of Devahuti
Transcendental Teachings of Prahlāda Mahārāja
Teachings of Queen Kuntī
Kṛṣṇa, the Reservoir of Pleasure
The Path of Perfection
Life Comes from Life
Message of Godhead
The Perfection of Yoga
Beyond Birth and Death
On the Way to Kṛṣṇa
Rāja-vidyā: The King of Knowledge
Elevation to Kṛṣṇa Consciousness
Kṛṣṇa Consciousness: The Matchless Gift
The Nārada-bhakti-sūtra (with disciples)
The Mukunda-mālā-stotra (with disciples)
Introduction to Bhagavad-gītā
Back to Godhead magazine (founder)
A Second Chance
The Journey of Self-Discovery
The Laws of Nature
Renunciation Through Wisdom
Civilization & Transcendence
The Quest for Enlightenment
Beyond Illusion and Doubt
Dharma: The Way of Transcendence
The Hare Krishna Challenge

A complete catalogue is available upon request. Please contact The Bhaktivedanta Book Trust, Hare Krishna Land, Juhu, Mumbai 400 049. The above books are also available at ISKCON centers.

Please contact a center near to your place.

BASICS OF BHAGAVAD-GITA

(A thematic study of Bhagavad-gītā)

Based on the teachings of
His Divine Grace
A.C.Bhaktivedanta Swami Prabhupāda
Founder-*Ācārya* of the International Society for Krishna Consciousness

The Bhaktivedanta Book Trust

Readers interested in the subject matter of this book are invited by The Bhaktivedanta Book Trust to correspond with its secretary at the following address:

The Bhaktivedanta Book Trust
Hare Krishna Land, Juhu,
Mumbai 400 049, India

Web / E-mail :
www.indiabbt.com
admin@indiabbt.com

Basics of Bhagavad-gītā (English)

1st Printing, July 2018 : 14,000 copies

ISBN: 978-93-86956-69-9

Published and Printed by
The Bhaktivedanta Book Trust.

SJ1K

Dedicated to

His Divine Grace A.C.Bhaktivedanta Swami Prabhupāda

Founder-*Ācārya* of the International Society for Krishna Consciousness

About Srila Prabhupāda

His Divine Grace A.C.Bhaktivedanta Swami Prabhupāda appeared in this world in 1896 in Calcutta, India. He first met his spiritual master, Śrīla Bhaktisiddhānta Sarasvatī Gosvāmi, in Calcutta in 1922. Bhaktisiddhānta Sarasvatī, a prominent religious scholar and the founder of sixty-four Gauḍīya Maṭhas (Vedic Institutes), liked this educated young man and convinced him to dedicate his life to teaching Vedic knowledge. Śrīla Prabhupāda became his student and, in 1933, his formally initiated disciple.

At their first meeting, in 1922, Śrīla Bhaktisiddhānta Sarasvatī requested Śrīla Prabhupāda to broadcast Vedic knowledge in English. In the years that followed, Śrīla Prabhupāda wrote a commentary on the *Bhagavad-gītā*, assisted the Gauḍīya Maṭha in its work, and, in 1944, started *Back to Godhead*, an English fortnightly magazine. Single- handedly, Śrīla Prabhupāda edited it, typed the manuscripts, checked the galley proofs, and even distributed the individual copies. The magazine is now being continued by his disciples all over the world.

In 1950 Śrīla Prabhupāda retired from married life, adopting the *vānaprastha* (retired) order to devote more time to his studies and writing.

He travelled to the holy city of Vṛndāvana, where he lived in humble circumstances in the historic temple of Rādhā-Dāmodara. There he engaged for several years in deep study and writing. He accepted the renounced order of life (*sannyāsa*) in 1959. At Rādhā-Dāmodara temple, Śrīla Prabhupāda began work on his life's masterpiece: a multivolume commentated translation of the eighteen-thousand verse *Śrīmad-Bhāgavatam* (*Bhāgavata Purāṇa*). He also wrote *Easy Journey to Other Planets*.

After publishing three volumes of the *Bhāgavatam*, Śrīla Prabhupāda came to the United States, in September 1965, to fulfill the mission of his spiritual master. Subsequently, His Divine Grace wrote more than fifty volumes of authoritative commentated translations and summary studies of the philosophical and religious classics of India.

When he first arrived by freighter in New York City, Śrīla Prabhupāda was practically penniless. Only after almost a year of great difficulty did he establish the International Society for Krishna Consciousness, in July of 1966. Before he passed away on November 14, 1977, he had guided the Society and seen it grow to a worldwide confederation of more than one hundred *āśramas*, schools, temples, institutes, and farm communities.

In 1972 His Divine Grace introduced the Vedic system of primary and secondary education in the West by founding gurukula school in Dallas, Texas. Since then his disciples have established similar schools throughout the United Stated and the rest of the world.

Śrīla Prabhupāda also inspired the construction of several large international cultural centers in India. The center at Śrīdhāma Māyāpur is the site for a planned spiritual city, an ambitious project for which construction will extend over many years to come. In Vṛndāvana are the magnificient Kṛṣṇa-Balarāma Temple and International Guesthouse, gurukula school, and Śrīla Prabhupāda Memorial and Mueseum. There is also a major cultural and educational center in Bombay. Other centers are planned in a dozen important locations on the Indian subcontinent.

Śrīla Prabhupāda's most significant contribution, however, is his books. Highly respected by scholars for their authority, depth, and clarity, they are used as textbooks in numerous college courses. His writings have been translated into over fifty languages. The Bhaktivedanta Book Trust, established in 1972 to publish the works of His Divine Grace, has thus become the world's largest publisher of books in the field of Indian religion and philosophy.

In just twelve years, in spite of his advanced age, Śrīla Prabhupāda circled the globe 14 times on lecture tours that took him to six continents. In spite of such a vigorous schedule, Śrīla Prabhupāda continued to write prolifically. His writings constitute a veritable library of Vedic philosophy, religion, literature, and culture.

PREFACE

The *Bhagavad-gītā* is undoubtedly one of the greatest spiritual texts the world has known. Spoken in the dramatic background of a battlefield setting, the *Bhagavad-gītā* explores the most fundamental and important ideas relevant for humanity, in a dialogue format.As the great Pandava warrior Arjuna finds himself bewildered at the onset of the war with his cousins, the Kauravas, his dear friend and guide, Kṛṣṇa, dispels his illusions with a clear explanation of spiritual truths, and indeed, also of this world.

Despite the popularity of the *Bhagavad-gītā* and its numerous translations and editions, it remains a mysterious text, with many people finding it difficult to decipher it. The reason is that these editions mostly take the reader away from the speaker of the text - Lord Kṛṣṇa.

The very term "*Bhagavad-gītā*" meaning "Song of God", indicates that the speaker, Kṛṣṇa, is God. But many commentators give some imaginary interpretation for this simple truth by saying, for example, that it is not Kṛṣṇa who is speaking but rather it is "the unborn within Kṛṣṇa" that is speaking, thus rendering a completely different meaning than intended.

The message of the book needs to be understood directly, or as it is, rather than through such speculative theories. A direct approach makes the text simple and the real meaning emerges. A speculative approach, however scholarly the commentator may be, can only take the reader away from the real meaning, thus leading to confusion.

So, when Kṛṣṇa says in the *Bhagavad-gītā*, "I am the Supreme", there is no need for speculation. We take that statement to mean exactly what it means, that is, that Kṛṣṇa is Supreme, that is all. It is as simple as that.

It is based on this principle that His Divine Grace A.C. Bhaktivedanta Swami Śrīla Prabhupāda, the Founder *Ācārya* of the International Society for Krishna Consciousness (ISKCON), wrote his translation and commentary of the *Bhagavad-gītā*. Deliberately and appropriately, he titled it "*Bhagavad-gītā As It Is*", to indicate that he followed the direct approach. This makes the book easy to understand and brings out the essence of Lord Kṛṣṇa's message of devotion clearly.

This book, "*Basics of Bhagavad-gītā*" is based on the "*Bhagavad-gītā As It Is*" in particular, and the teachings of Śrīla Prabhupāda in general.

We have preferred to adopt a thematic approach in this book that you now hold in your hands. What exactly is this 'thematic approach'? It is an approach where the subject matter is presented concept-wise, rather than chapter-wise.

There are many concepts given in the *Bhagavad-gītā* and it is essential to understand them properly and clearly. However, these concepts are spread throughout the book with Lord Kṛṣṇa referring to them according to the questions Arjuna asks. To make it easier for the reader, we have, thus put together these concepts, drawing from different sections of the book.
As you read the Table of Contents, you will see how this categorization of concepts has been done.

We have also, from time to time, made references to certain ideas and theories that are prevalent in the modern age, and analyzed them from the perspective of the *Bhagavad-gītā*.

We have tried to make the subject as simple as possible, and yet clear and substantial. We hope you will find this useful in your journey to spiritual success and happiness. We wish you well on this exciting voyage. May Lord Kṛṣṇa bless you with success on this path.

Please note that since it is hard to convey the correct pronunciation, and even the right alphabet of the Sanskrit language in the English script, we have adopted, for the Sanskrit verses and terms, the format used in scholarly circles. Please find a description of this format in the "Sanskrit Pronunciation Guide" at the end of this book.

TABLE OF CONTENTS

1. INTRODUCTION

Rescuing Sītā
Introduction to Bhagavad-gītā
Elevation to Kṛṣṇa Consciousness
Perfect Questions Perfect Answers
KṚṢṆA
Teachings of Lord Caitanya
ŚRĪMAD BHĀGAVATAM
ŚRĪMAD BHĀGAVATAM
Teachings of Queen Kuntī
The Journey of Self-Discovery
LIFE COMES FROM LIFE
The Matchless Gift
THE NECTAR OF INSTRUCTION
Lord Caitanya
A Beginner's Guide to Kṛṣṇa Consciousness
THE PATH OF PERFECTION
ŚRĪ CAITANYA CARITĀMṚTA
ŚRĪLA PRABHUPĀDA LĪLĀMṚTA
BEYOND BIRTH & DEATH
ORIGINS
A Beginner's Guide to Kṛṣṇa Consciousness
KṚṢṆA
KṚṢṆA
BHAGAVAD-GĪTĀ AS IT IS
Darśana
Yoga
The Nectar of Devotion
The Hare Kṛṣṇa Challenge
BHAGAVAD-GĪTĀ AS IT IS
The Laws of Nature
ŚRĪMAD BHĀGAVATAM
Chant and be Happy
MESSAGE OF GODHEAD
The Matchless Gift
TEACHINGS OF LORD CAITANYA
ŚRĪ ĪŚOPANIṢAD
THE PATH OF PERFECTION
ŚRĪMAD BHĀGAVATAM

CHAPTER 1

INTRODUCTION

1.1 WHAT IS BHAGAVAD-GĪTĀ?

■ *Bhagavad-gītā* was spoken five thousand years ago by Lord Kṛṣṇa to His friend and devotee, Arjuna. This great historical event occurred before the onset of Mahābhārata war between the Kauravas and Pāṇḍavas on the battlefield of Kurukṣetra.

■ *Bhagavad-gītā* is a classic of timeless wisdom, the summum bonum of spiritual truth. It has deeply influenced the thinking of generations of philosophers, theologians, educators, scientists and authors all over the world.

■ *Bhagavad-gītā* originally appears in the form of 700 Sanskrit verses, as an episode of the *Mahābhārata*, a great historical epic, in which it occupies chapters 25 through 42 in the *Bhīṣma Parva*. The author of *Mahābhārata* is the great sage Vyāsadeva, "the literary incarnation of God." Vyāsadeva, after completing the four principal *Vedas*, the *Upaniṣads* and the *Vedānta-sūtra*, decided to compile the *Purāṇas*, and the *Mahābhārata* for the benefit of common people who could not sufficiently assimilate the lofty philosophical teachings of the earlier works.

■ *Bhagavad-gītā* is the essence of all Vedic Knowledge and is one of the most important *Upaniṣads* in Vedic literature.

1.2. WHAT IS ITS PURPOSE?

I) To deliver mankind from ignorance

Every man is in difficulty in so many ways, as Arjuna was in difficulty in having to fight the battle of Kurukṣetra. Arjuna, forgetful of his

prescribed duties as a *kṣatriya* (warrior), whose duty is to fight for a righteous cause in a holy war, decides for personally motivated reasons (illusion), not to fight.

Lord Kṛṣṇa , who has agreed to act as the driver of Arjuna's chariot, sees His friend and devotee in illusion and perplexity. He then proceeds to enlighten Arjuna regarding his immediate social duty (*Varna dharma*) as a warrior and more important, his eternal duty or nature (*Sanātana-dharma*) as a spirit soul.

II) To revive the eternal relationship of love between each Soul and God

Kṛṣṇa speaks for the benefit of all souls, who have forgotten their eternal nature and their eternal relationship of love with Him. To revive this relationship is the ultimate goal of our existence.

1.3. WHY SHOULD ONE TRY TO UNDERSTAND BHAGAVAD-GĪTĀ?

I) The human form of life is special

There are four activities common to humans and animals - eating, sleeping, mating and defending.

āhāra-nidrā-bhaya-maithunaṁ ca
samānam etat paśubhir narāṇām
dharmo hi teṣām adhiko viśeṣo
dharmeṇa hīnaḥ paśubhiḥ samānāḥ
(*Hitopadeśa*)

Translation: "*The activities of eating, sleeping, mating and defending are common in animals and human beings. The human beings are considered superior only when they inquire about the Absolute Truth, otherwise they are considered as good as animals.*"

Human beings have the special prerogative of possessing reasoning power, of inquiring about their position and so on.

Unless one is awakened to this position of questioning one's suffering, one is not a perfect human being.

EATING

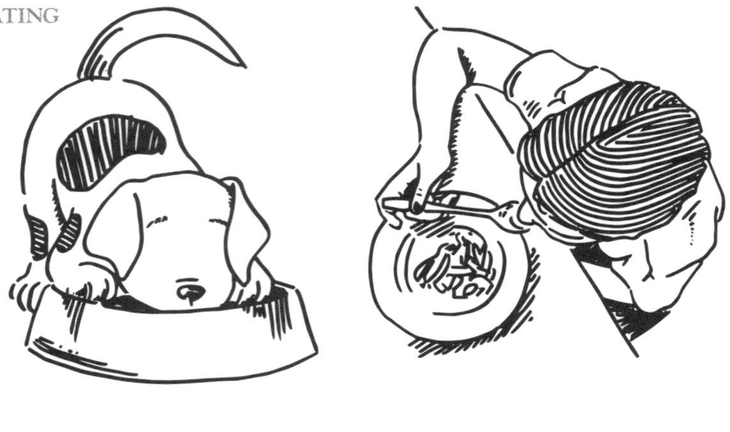

MATING

SLEEPING

DEFENDING

We do not want heat, cold, thirst, hunger, birth, old age, disease and death. But nobody is free from all these sufferings. Everyone is full of anxiety whether he admits it or not.

II) To make a permanent solution to the suffering in this world

After attaining the human form of birth, we are subject to three kinds of material miseries:

- adhyātmic: Miseries caused by our own body and mind
- adhibhautic: Miseries caused by other living entities (mosquitoes etc.)
- adhidaivic: Disturbance caused by natural disasters (earthquakes, famines etc.)

Therefore, those who begin to question why they are suffering or where they came from and where they shall go after death, are proper students for understanding *Bhagavad-gītā*. The *Bhagavad-gītā* says that out of many thousands someone may develop this reasoning power of inquiring, "Why am I suffering?" Kṛṣṇa spoke *Bhagavad-gītā* to answer these questions and relieve Arjuna and us from all miseries of material life by imparting the highest spiritual knowledge.

1.4. HOW SHOULD ONE UNDERSTAND THE BHAGAVAD-GĪTĀ?

I) Not as a mythological story, but as a true, historical event.

II) One should accept the *Bhagavad-gītā* "as it is" i.e. without twisting the meaning to suit our liking.

III) "*Bhagavad-gītā*" means "song of God", so, one should accept the speaker, Lord Kṛṣṇa, as God, at least theoretically in the beginning.

IV) "*Bhagavad-gītā*" should be understood in a spirit of devotion. Otherwise, it will be like a bee licking the outside of a bottle of honey. One cannot have the taste of honey unless one opens the bottle. Similarly, the spiritual wisdom and mysticism of the *Bhagavad-gītā* can be understood only by the devotees and not by others. Nor can the *Bhagavad-gītā* be touched by persons who envy the very existence of the Lord.

1.5. WHAT IS THE SUBJECT MATTER DISCUSSED IN BHAGAVAD-GĪTĀ?

The *Bhagavad-gītā* essentially deals with the following five topics:

I) ***Īśvara*** (god)

II) ***Jīva*** (spirit soul)

III) ***Prakṛti*** (material nature)

IV) ***Kāla*** (time)

V) ***Karma*** (activity)

ĪŚVARA (GOD)

JĪVA (SPIRIT SOUL)

PRAKṚTI (MATERIAL NATURE)

KĀLA (TIME)

KARMA (ACTIVITY)

DISCIPLIC SUCCESSION (GURU-ŚIṢYA PARAMPARĀ)

1.6. WHO CAN UNDERSTAND BHAGAVAD-GĪTĀ? (I.E. WHAT ARE THE QUALIFICATIONS OF A DISCIPLE?)

I) One must be inquisitive about the ultimate goal of life.

II) One must approach a bona fide spiritual master and surrender unto him.

tasmād gurum prapadyeta
jijñāsuḥ śreya uttamam
śābde pare ca niṣṇātaṁ
brahmaṇy upaśamāśrayam
(***Śrīmad-Bhāgavatam*** **11.3.21**)

Translation: *"Therefore any person who seriously desires real happiness must seek a bona fide spiritual master and take shelter of him by initiation. The qualification of the bona fide guru is that he has realized the conclusions of the scriptures by deliberation and is able to convince others of these conclusions. Such great personalities, who have taken shelter of the Supreme Godhead, leaving aside all material considerations, should be understood to be bona fide spiritual masters."*

III) One must inquire submissively and hear attentively from the *guru*.

IV) One must render service to the *guru* and please him.

tad viddhi praṇipātena
paripraśnena sevayā
upadekṣyanti te jñānaṁ
jñāninas tattva-darśinaḥ
(***Bhagavad-gītā*** 4.34)

Translation: *"Just try to learn the truth by approaching a spiritual master. Inquire from him submissively and render service unto him.*

The self-realized souls can impart knowledge unto you because they have seen the truth."

V) One must have faith in the *guru*

yasya deve parā bhaktir
yathā deve tathā gurau
tasyaite kathitā hy arthāḥ
prakāśante mahātmanaḥ
(*Svetasvatara Upanishad* 6.38)

Translation: *"Only unto those great souls who have implicit faith in both the Lord and the spiritual master are all the imports of Vedic knowledge automatically revealed."*

VI) One must be a devotee of the Lord

sa evāyaṁ mayā te 'dya
yogaḥ proktaḥ purātanaḥ
bhakto 'si me sakhā ceti
rahasyaṁ hy etad uttamam
(*Bhagavad-gītā* 4.3)

Translation: *"That very ancient science of the relationship with the Supreme is today told by Me to you because you are My devotee as well as My friend and can therefore understand the transcendental mystery of this science."*

1.7. FROM WHOM SHOULD ONE UNDERSTAND BHAGAVAD-GĪTĀ? (I.E. WHAT ARE THE QUALIFICATIONS OF A GURU?)

I) He must be in a disciplic succession (*guru-śiṣya paramparā*) coming from God Himself.

evaṁ paramparā-prāptam
imaṁ rājarṣayo viduḥ
sa kāleneha mahatā
yogo naṣṭaḥ parantapa
(*Bhagavad-gītā* 4.2)

Translation: *"This supreme science was thus received through the chain of disciplic succession, and the saintly kings understood it in that way. But in course of time the succession was broken, and therefore the science as it is appears to be lost."*

II) Like a Postman, he must deliver the divine message "as it is", without speculation or concoction.

III) He must have realized the conclusions of the scriptures by deliberation.

tasmād guruṁ prapadyeta
jijñāsuḥ śreya uttamam
śābde pare ca niṣṇātaṁ
brahmaṇy upaśamāśrayam
(*Śrīmad-Bhāgavatam* 11.3.21)

Translation: *"Therefore any person who seriously desires real happiness must seek a bona fide spiritual master and take shelter of him by initiation. The qualification of the bona fide guru is that he has realized the conclusions of the scriptures by deliberation and is able to convince others of these conclusions. Such great personalities, who have taken shelter of the Supreme Godhead, leaving aside all material considerations, should be understood to be bona fide spiritual masters."*

IV) The teachings of the *guru* must be in conformity with the teachings of the previous *guru* in the *paramparā* and with the scriptures

Spiritual teachings must stand firmly on the tripod of *guru*, sādhu (previous *ācāryas*) and *śāstra* (scripture).

V) He must practice what he preaches i.e. he must have the proper '*ācaran*'. Such a person is therefore called *Ācārya*.

VI) He must be fixed in devotional service of the Lord.

VII) His senses must be controlled.

vāco vegaṁ manasaḥ krodha-vegaṁ
jihvā-vegam udaropastha-vegam
etān vegān yo viṣaheta dhīraḥ
sarvām apīmāṁ pṛthivīṁ sa śiṣyāt
(*Upadeśāmṛta* 1)

Translation: "*A sober person who can tolerate the urge to speak, the mind's demands, the actions of anger and the urges of the tongue, belly and genitals is qualified to make disciples all over the world.*"

VIII) He must see all living beings with equal vision and must be their well-wisher. He must be a friend of all and hate no one.

vidyā-vinaya-sampanne
brāhmaṇe gavi hastini
śuni caiva śva-pāke ca
paṇḍitāḥ sama-darśinaḥ
(*Bhagavad-gītā* 5.18)

Translation: "*The humble sages, by virtue of true knowledge, see with equal vision a learned and gentle brāhmaṇa, a cow, an elephant, a dog and a dog-eater (outcaste).*"

His Divine Grace A. C. Bhaktivedanta Swami Prabhupāda Founder *Ācārya* of ISKCON is one outstanding example of an ideal spiritual master in our modern times.

1.8. THE THREE STEPS TO PERFECTION

By the study of *Bhagavad-gītā*, it is possible to understand:

I) Who is God? What is the relationship between God and the soul? This is called '*Sambandha*'.

II) Process of reviving the soul's relationship with God. This is called '*Abhidheya*'.

III) Attainment of love of God, which is the ultimate goal of life. This is called '*Prayojana*'.

1.9. TWO PROCESSES OF ACQUIRING KNOWLEDGE

- Modern science has absolutely no understanding of the first two of the five subjects of ***Bhagavad-gītā*** (***Īśvara*** and ***Jīva***) and very limited and imperfect understanding of the last three subjects (***Prakṛti, Kāla and Karma***).

- This is because the very process of acquiring knowledge that it follows is defective. It is called the 'ascending' or inductive process ('*āroha-panthā*').

- The inductive or ascending process means to not accept any authority and to try to find out truth by one's own endeavor and speculation.

DEDUCTIVE PROCESS

INDUCTIVE PROCESS

- **Consider the following two examples:**

a) If someone wants to find out who his father is, and if he tries to do it by research and experimentation, by surveying the male population, that is inductive process.

b) When told that "Man is mortal", if someone wants to research and verify this statement, that is again, the inductive process.

- **As opposed to the inductive or ascending process, is the 'deductive' or 'descending' process ('*avaroha-panthā*').**

- **The deductive or the descending process means to accept a bona fide authority and learn the truth by inquiring from that authority.**

- **Consider again the same two examples given above:**

a) To find out who one's father is, the simple way is to ask one's mother. The power of her authority in terms of reliability of information is greater than all sources of evidence. This is the deductive process.

b) When told that "man is mortal", we accept it. We do not experiment unnecessarily. This is the deductive process.

- **The inductive process is always fraught with uncertainty and inaccuracy.**

- **Scriptures like the *Bhagavad-gītā* are the perfect authority from which we can acquire perfect knowledge, because they are the word of God. This is the simple and straightforward method to obtain true knowledge.**

1.10. WHAT IS "PROOF"?

- **Even though the deductive process is simple and straightforward by nature, people in general do not wish to accept it.** When confronted with words like "God", "scripture", "soul", etc, they ask: "What is the proof of this?" Or "Show me God".

- **People use words like "proof" or "evidence" very lightly without knowing what these words really mean.**

- **The first question to ask in response is "To whom shall we 'prove?"** To understand the 'proof' for something, we need to be qualified. For example, to understand the proof for some complex mathematical formula, first of all, we need to be trained in mathematics. Then only can one understand the "proof". Similarly, we need to be properly trained in spiritual knowledge before we become qualified to understand the "Proofs" for spiritual topics.

- **The next question to ask is, "What kind of proof do you seek?"** There are different kinds of 'proofs'. Is the proof of 'seeing with your own eyes', the proof that you seek? By that standard many things in life and nature cannot be proven.

- **The *Vedas* say that there are basically three kinds of 'proof'.** The Sanskrit word for 'proof 'or 'evidence' is "***pramāṇa***". The three kinds of ***pramāṇa*** are:

  - ***pratyakṣa pramāṇa***
  - ***anumāna pramāṇa***
  - ***śabda pramāṇa***

1.11. THREE KINDS OF PROOF (PRAMĀṆA)

I) *Pratyakṣa pramāṇa*

This is the knowledge obtained by direct perception through our senses. Majority of scientific experiments and proofs are based on the principle, "Seeing is believing" which is a famous dictum of people arguing about God's existence. But we can give many simple counter arguments to defeat this misconception.

- **Is the sun just a plate of half-a-meter diameter as we see it with our eyes?**
- **A stick appears broken when we insert half of it into water (Refraction).**
- **Why do our faces look like that of a ghost in a concave mirror? (Is seeing believing?!!!).**

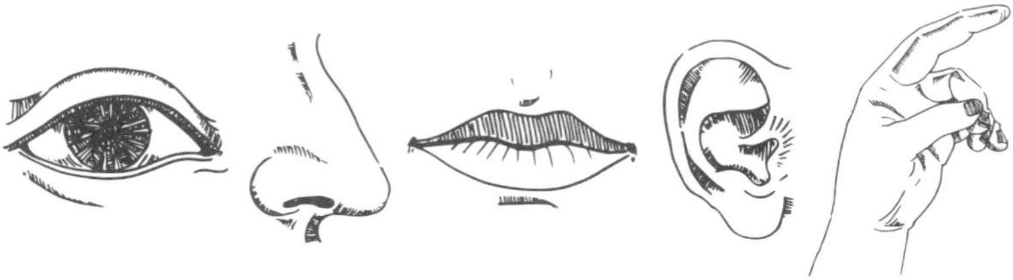

We understand that direct perception by our senses is not a very reliable method because the sense organs themselves have only a limited range. We cannot acquire absolute knowledge through the material senses and mind, and any knowledge thus derived will be relative only.

The very fact that the information and theories in science are changed, updated and modified everyday is proof that we are attaining higher and higher imperfect relative truths by the pursuit of our scientific research.

The Absolute Truth however, is fixed. It never changes. The reason we cannot understand the Absolute Truth through our blunt material senses is that we have the following four defects:

A) OUR SENSES ARE IMPERFECT:

Our senses (eyes, ears, nose etc.) have a very limited range of perception.

For example, we cannot see objects below a certain size or in insufficient light. Scientific instruments can simply increase the power of the senses but not replace them. And ultimately however sophisticated these instruments are, knowledge comes to us through our senses, which are imperfect.

B) TENDENCY TO BE ILLUSIONED:

All our senses are subject to many deceptions.

For example, carbonated water tastes colder than ordinary water at the same temperature; orange tastes sour after tasting sugar, but after tasting a lemon it tastes sweet.

We are all aware of mirages in the desert and other such optical illusions.

C) TENDENCY TO COMMIT MISTAKES:

"To err is human," the saying goes. The scientists are no exception!

For example, science considered ticks to be the smallest living creatures till microbes were discovered; Stars were thought to be pinpricks in a crystal globe and so on.

D) TENDENCY TO CHEAT:

Humans also go beyond innocent errors and deliberately propagate untruths or fabricate evidence for some personal gain.

In science, the Piltdown Man hoax is well known.

II) *Anumāna pramāṇa*

- This is the knowledge arrived by making hypothesis or inference based on ***pratyakṣa pramāṇa.***

- For example, upon hearing a loud crashing sound in the next room, we may infer that a flower vase has broken. We cannot immediately know with certainty what has actually happened.

- *Anumāna pramāṇa* is also unreliable because it relies on our faulty sense perception. Thus, it cannot independently lead to perfect knowledge. Charles Darwin's 'Theory of evolution', much of archaeology and other sciences rely upon such speculation ("it may have been like this" or "perhaps it is like this").

We are all familiar with the story of the six blind men and the elephant.

BLIND MEN AND THE ELEPHANT

Once upon a time, six blind men came across an elephant for the first time in their life.

After touching different parts of the elephant, each one of them was very enthusiastic to describe what the elephant was like.

One man touched the side of the elephant and exclaimed, "It is like a wall".

The second man touched the tusk and said, "Oh! It is so very round, smooth and sharp, the elephant is like a spear!"

The third man touched the trunk and said, "Don't you understand that the elephant is like a snake?"

The fourth man grasped one of the legs of the elephant and felt that the elephant was like a tree.

The fifth man touched one of the ears of the elephant and said that it was like a fan.

The sixth man caught hold of the swinging tail of the elephant and said, "Why don't you understand that the elephant is like a rope!"

In this way they went on arguing until they resorted to the help of a learned man with broad, open eyes. The learned man felt pity on them and told them the exact description of the elephant and then all the six blind men became completely satisfied.

Just like the endeavor of the six blind men, our endeavor to understand the material world or the Absolute Truth with our defective senses and inferences will not yield us correct and complete knowledge. Sometimes we may grab a particular part of the truth, although it may be correct; but it does not give us the complete truth.

III) *Śabda pramāṇa*

- This is knowledge or evidence obtained by hearing from a bona fide authority.
- In our daily life we often accept many things as true, of which we have no first-hand knowledge, simply because they are spoken by an authority. For example, we accept that there is a country called "Ghana" in Africa, even though we may have never been there, because our geography text books say so; or we may accept that the atoms consist of electrons and protons although we have never seen them.
- Of course these authorities, being imperfect, give us imperfect or incomplete knowledge. However, the principle of hearing from an authority holds.

- Accepting information from a bona fide authority is thus beneficial and necessary because:

a. We have no choice
b. It saves time and inconvenience
c. It is safe

- If this is so for ordinary subjects of the world, how much more should it hold for spiritual subjects like God, soul etc., which are beyond the range of our ordinary material senses.

- God cannot be understood by our blunt material senses or our intellectual capacity. God can be understood only when He reveals Himself through the scripture and through great saintly persons who live according to scripture.

- When we say "*śabda pramāṇa*", we refer to that authority which is infallible, perfect and free from all defects. Who is such an authority? It is God alone. By definition, then, only God can truly give us knowledge that is free from defects.

- The word of God is "Scripture". It is "*apauruṣeya*" because it has a divine origin. It is complete knowledge and is thus called "*Veda*".

- The Vedic knowledge comes down in disciplic succession of great saintly persons and is available even today.

- The Vedic truths are 'axiomatic' truths i.e., when something is stated in the *Vedas,* we immediately accept it as truth. The evidence for it being true is that it appears in the *Veda*. That's all. This is *śabda pramāṇa* - the highest evidence.

- Sometimes we may think that Vedic knowledge is not true because it appears to conflict with what our senses perceive. But our senses, as we have seen, are not at all reliable sources of evidence, and we should, therefore, still accept the Vedic conclusions.

- An example of how Vedic axiomatic truth is really true, although it appears to conflict with our common sense is the case of cow dung. The dung of all animals is considered impure but cow dung is stated to be very pure in the *Vedas*. Modern tests have proven this beyond doubt.
- We should not think that accepting Vedic knowledge, as axiomatic truth is "blind faith", as is the common misconception. It is, in fact, the ultimate knowledge because it is the word of the God.
- When one practices the recommendations of the scripture one finds that they 'work' and thus it is a science.
- In any case, all knowledge, ordinary or spiritual, depends on faith in something or someone; therefore, by putting our faith on the highest authority, God, we can gain the ultimate benefit of life.
- If a child wants to know who his father, is, he simply has to ask his mother, the natural authority. He does not have to make a survey of the male population. Similarly, accepting the highest authority, the Vedic knowledge, is the way to attain true knowledge and bliss.
- **Thus, among the three kinds of evidence or sources of knowledge, "*śabda pramāṇa*" is the best because it is authorized, reliable, free from defects and capable of revealing the Absolute Truth.**

1.12. SOME EXAMPLES OF THE INFALLIBLE WISDOM OF THE VEDIC SCRIPTURE

King Pṛthu chases the Earth (krishna.com)

Formerly, the earth was considered flat, until modern science revealed that it was somewhat spherical. The *Vedas* have stated long ago that the earth is round – "Bhūgol".

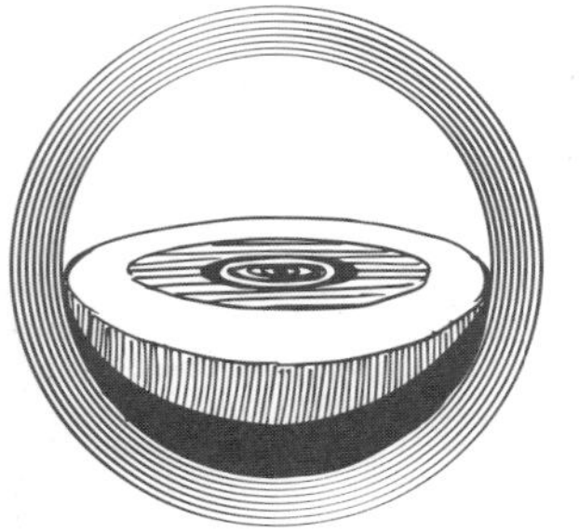

Bhū-maṇḍala with 7 islands (Bhaktivedanta Vidyapitha)

The *Vedas* also speak about "Sapta-dvīpa", the seven islands; long before modern geography understood the seven continents.

Albert Einstein (Pixabay.com)

The concept of "relativity of Time" has entered into modern science only about a century or so ago. But the *Vedas* have talked about it in great detail thousands of years ago.

- The Vedic scriptures have made many predictions about events and people in the distant future. Some examples are Gautama Buddha (*Śrīmad-Bhāgavatam* 1.3.24), Cāṇakya and Chandragupta Maurya (*Śrīmad-Bhāgavatam* 12.1.11). The above examples can help us develop faith in the holy Vedic scriptures.

1.13. WHAT IS SCRIPTURE?

Having understood what '*Śabda pramāṇa*' is, we can now answer the question, "What is Scripture?" The Scripture is:

A) The word of God

- It is not mythology, or the concoction of the fertile brain of some imaginative authors, but directly the word of God.

B) The law book of life

- Just as the law books of the country govern our life as citizens of the country, similarly, the *Vedas* govern our life as human beings. Just as lawyers quote from their law books while they argue their case in the court, followers of the *Vedas* quote the Vedic scriptures as evidence.

C) A manual for the universe

- Just as the manufacturer of a TV set supplies an instruction manual to the buyer along with the T.V, similarly, God, the creator of the universe, has given us a manual - the *Veda* – to tell us how to use the things in the world and how to live in it.

D) The means to understand God

- A child need only ask its mother about who its father is. Similarly, one need only refer to the Vedic scripture in order to understand who God is.
- Thus God is like our father and the scripture is like our mother.
- God reveals Himself through the medium of the *Vedas*.

E) Absolute knowledge

- Knowledge obtained by our senses in this world (*pratyakṣa pramāṇa* and *anumāna pramāṇa*) is relative knowledge because it is imperfect and ever changing.
- People who try to understand the world through their senses alone, are like the six blind men (referred to earlier) who tried to understand an elephant, each by touching a different part of the elephant and coming to the conclusion that the part they touched was the complete elephant.
- As opposed to this, *śabda pramāṇa*, or the Vedic scripture, presents knowledge that is infallible, perfect and free from defects. Thus, it is absolute knowledge.
- Absolute knowledge does not change with time, place and circumstance. For example, the *Vedas* tell us that we are eternal spirit soul, the *ātma*. This holds good for all living beings in all places and at all times. In contrast, the modern conception of 'personality' or 'identity' has changed over the years.

F) Perfect science

- It is not simply 'blind faith' or 'Dogma'
- It is actually a very subtle and perfect science that can be understood, practiced and verified.
- It is a common misconception that spiritual truths cannot be verified. Modern scientists err when they try to impose the methodology of modern science upon this spiritual science to verify spiritual truths. Thus they say that spiritual knowledge is not a science.
- Spiritual truths, however, can certainly be verified but by another, more refined methodology that is outlined in the Vedic scripture itself. Vedic truths, thus, have to be understood on their own terms and not otherwise, just as modern science has its own pre-defined assumptions and methodology.

1.14. WHAT ARE THE VEDAS?

- The ***Vedas*** are a very ancient body of knowledge and are the word of the God. ***Veda*** means "the aggregate of knowledge."
- Before Vyāsadeva compiled the Vedic literatures, the latter was simply heard and the disciples would imbibe the knowledge by hearing.
- Later on Vyāsadeva thought it wise to write down the *Vedas* because in this age (Kali Yuga) people have short memories and are unable to remember Vedic instructions.
- Therefore, he compiled the four *Vedas* - *Sāma*, *Yajur*, *Ṛg*, *Atharva*, the 108 *Upaniṣads*, the 18 *Purāṇas*, the *Vedānta-sūtra*, the *Mahābhārata* and many others.
- These revealed scriptures are considered the standard books to be understood by human society.

VEDAS

- FOUR VEDAS
- UPANIṢADS
- VEDĀNTA SŪTRA
- PURĀṆAS
- ITIHĀSAS
- OTHERS

- The *Vedas* can thus be classified into various categories.

- *Bhagavad-gītā* is also known as the *Gītopaniṣad*, and is considered the Fifth *Veda*. This is stated in scriptures like the *Chāndogya Upaniṣad* and *Bhaviṣya Purāṇa*.

sarvopaniṣado gāvo
dogdhā gopāla-nandanaḥ
pārtho vatsaḥ sudhīr bhoktā
dugdhaṁ gītāmṛtaṁ mahat
(*Gītā māhātmya* 6)

■ "This *Gītopaniṣad, Bhagavad-gītā*, the essence of all the *Upaniṣads*, is just like a cow, and Lord Kṛṣṇa, who is famous as a cowherd boy, is milking this cow. Arjuna is just like a calf, and learned scholars and pure devotees are to drink the nectarean milk of *Bhagavad-gītā*".

2.
GOD

CHAPTER 2

GOD

DOES GOD EXIST? WHO IS GOD?

2.1. COMMON ATHEISTIC ARGUMENTS

Whether God exists or not is a fundamental question facing mankind today. What was accepted commonly as a fact in the bygone ages is now being increasingly questioned.

- Some of the common arguments put forward by atheists are as follows:
- **What is the proof that He exists? If we can't see Him, why believe that He exists?** (This is the typical "frog-in-the well" attitude. There was once a frog that was born in a well and had lived there all his life. Another frog, which lived near the sea, visited this frog. The frog in the well tried to estimate the size of the sea by comparing it to the well, "is your house, the sea, twice the size of my well? Ten times? Hundred times?" The sea is actually far too vast for any such comparison. Because the first frog had never been outside his well, he tried to see everything in the world in terms of his very limited experience of the well. Similarly atheists try to speculate on matters pertaining to God on the basis of their very insignificant experience of this world and then arrive at faulty conclusions.)
- **The idea of 'God' was introduced to explain phenomena in nature, but science is now able to do that and one day science will fully explain everything. Thus there will be no need for 'God'.**
- **If God exists, why is there so much suffering? Why is He so cruel that He allows His children to suffer?**

■ **The idea of God has been introduced simply to ensure morality and good behavior in the society.**

In the present-day materialistic society, such atheistic ideas have become very widespread, and as a result much havoc has been caused to the world. Therefore, there is a great need to establish that God exists and that belief in God is actually very rational, logical and scientific.

2.2. LOGIC FOR BELIEF IN EXISTENCE OF GOD

I) Creation implies creator

While atheistic views are gaining in numbers, an examination of the world around us gives us a different story. Every part of the creation is a testimony to the presence of God.

Consider the following:

Every garden reveals its gardener, every clock its maker and every design its designer. Everyone will agree that a design means that a

designer is responsible for it. For example, let us take the watch on our wrist. It could not have come out of thin air but must have had a designer and an assembler behind it. Thus we cannot deny the existence of the personality who created the watch. **Similarly, the creation reveals its creator – God.**

The universe and everything within it is superbly organized. This indicates the existence of a superb organizer. If we look up at the stars and planets in the sky we will observe that their movements are so precise, that even watches can be set against these movements, day after day, year after year. How then can we deny the existence of a designer and assembler behind the universe?

Every organ of our body is very intricate and more complex than a computer. If a computer cannot come about by itself, how can a body, which is a perfect working assembly of such complex organs, come by chance? There must be a creator who has created all these wonderful things.

Sir Isaac Newton, though a scientist, was a believer in God. Once an atheistic scientist visited him. Newton showed him a new mechanical model of the sun and all the planets. He cranked a handle and all the planets revolved around the sun like in the universe. The scientist was very impressed and congratulated Newton on his achievement. Newton said he had not built the model but it had just appeared on its own without any human intervention one morning in his living room! When the scientist protested that this was not possible, Newton reprimanded him for believing otherwise, in the case of the real universe. He said: "You refuse to believe that this tiny model has come about by chance, yet you so readily accept that the actual solar system, with all its vastness and complexity, has no creator! Is this not highly illogical?

Indeed, the universe is so amazingly ordered and precise in it's working, it is like an enormous clock. What is more amazing than this amazing universe is that there are people who say it has no creator!

II) Law implies law-maker

Atheists may explain the orderly movements of planets in terms of Laws of nature. Yes, certainly, the universe is functioning according to natural laws. These laws work perfectly and without exception, but, scientists can, at best, discover that such laws exist.

The main point however is: who has made these laws? And who implements them?

Can the traffic signal on the road come about by itself?

Isn't it common sense that someone has laid down, that, 'red' means stop and 'green' means go and that someone (the police) is required to enforce these rules?

Therefore, we can understand that there must be a super-intelligent and powerful lawmaker behind the 'natural laws' in the universe.

III) Unseen thread in creation

In a pearl necklace, the pearls rest on a thread that ties them all together. Even though we cannot see the thread, we know that it

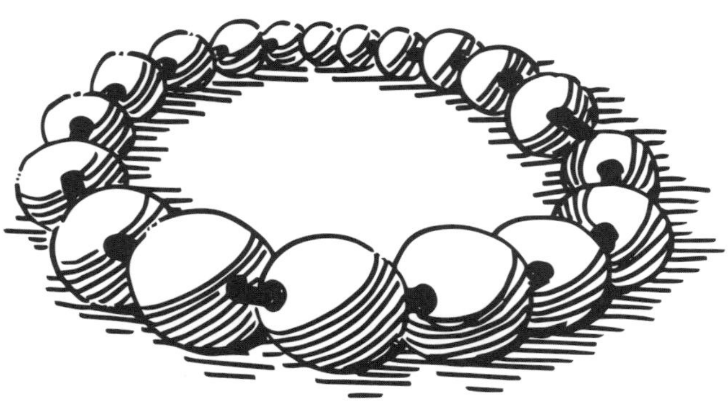

exists simply by seeing the pearls arranged in an orderly way, without being scattered.

Similarly, God is the underlying support of this universe, because of Whom, all the planets float and move in their perfect orbits, without falling down or crashing into each other.

In the *Bhagavad-gītā*, Lord Kṛṣṇa declares:

mattaḥ parataraṁ nānyat
kiñcid asti dhanañ-jaya
mayi sarvam idaṁ protaṁ
sūtre maṇi-gaṇā iva
(*Bhagavad gītā* - 7.7)

Translation: *"O conqueror of wealth, there is no truth superior to Me. Everything rests upon Me, as pearls are strung on a thread."*

God holds together the whole creation just as we would hold particles of dust in our palm.

IV) The idea of "Creation by chance" violates "Laws of nature"

It is a natural and empirically observed law that every system naturally moves from a state of order to disorder. We experience this in our daily lives. A great deal of effort is required to keep things in order in every sphere of our life. We have to put lot of effort simply to keep our house neat and tidy.

The universe is enormous and complex and is yet superbly ordered and harmonious. The very word 'COSMOS' means an "orderly, harmonious, systematic universe". From the atom, through the individual cells, organs, living entities right up to the gigantic universe - at every level there is incredible and stunning intricacy, beauty, and exquisite order.

It is illogical to assume that such a state of order has come about (and is being maintained) by chance, and without a background intelligence operating. This idea is against the nature's law that in a system left to itself, order gives way to disorder, and that to create or maintain order, an intelligent direction is required.

We have absolutely no experience of any object or system coming about by chance. Why and how then can we assume that the entire universe with all its harmony, order and structured organization came about by chance? It is important to understand that the word 'chance' does not actually refer to a cause – it refers to a certain type of pattern which is the result of an operation or activity repeated a sufficient number of times.

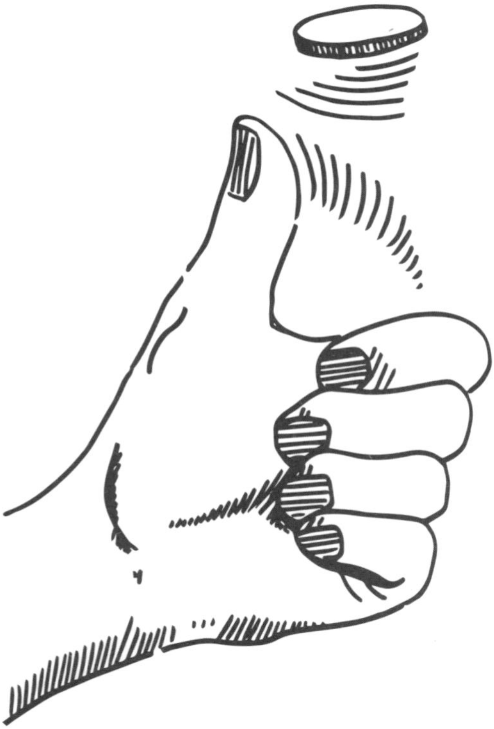

For example, we can toss a coin many times and note that the results correspond to a statistical pattern indicating a 50% probability that heads will turn up rather than tails. Therefore, the next time we toss a coin we could hazard a prediction that, based on the earlier pattern, there is a 50% chance (or likelihood) that it will turn up heads. But this does not mean that chance is the cause of the coin turning up heads. Each time the coin turns up head or tails, there is a cause or a combination of causes, which we may or may not be able to compute.

In other words, **"chance" is simply our estimation (made in advance) of likelihood of an event happening in a certain way, based on our observation on that event several times in the past.**

Turning our attention now to our universe, we can see that it is meaningless to talk about the universe coming about by chance, as if chance were the cause of the universe. And in any case, where is the question of even talking about chance when one is not in a position to observe the creation of the universe repeated a sufficient number of times to arrive at a pattern, like for tossing of coins? Furthermore, estimations of "chance" have to be made before the creation of the universe, not after.

So the universe HAS a cause, and that ultimate cause is God, the Supremely Intelligent Person.

V) Search for God is a fundamental urge

The existence of an urge indicates the existence of its fulfillment in nature, because nature is complete and perfect. For example, for the fulfillment of hunger and thirst, nature provides food and water.

Similarly the fundamental urge for God in all of us means that such a Supreme Being exists. Srila Prabhupāda said: "All are looking for God-some know it, some don't."

How true! Everyone is looking for happiness – but they don't know that real happiness lies in loving and serving God.

Everyone is looking for somebody to follow and worship – be it a cinema star, a sports star or some famous personality.

Everyone is looking for a hero.

God is the perfect and complete Hero. All desires can be fulfilled by worshipping Him.

VI) Personal experience of God

God is not just some abstract, intangible entity simply to be argued about. He is actually to be realized by the process of love and service in the company of His devotees. This knowledge is the topmost knowledge by understanding which full realization can be attained. Lord Kṛṣṇa says in the *Bhagavad-gītā*:

rāja-vidyā rāja-guhyaṁ
pavitram idam uttamam
pratyakṣāvagamaṁ dharmyaṁ
su-sukhaṁ kartum avyayam

(*Bhagavad-gītā* 9.2)

Translation: "*This knowledge is the king of education, the most secret of all secrets. It is the purest knowledge, and because it gives direct perception of the self by realization, it is the perfection of religion. It is everlasting, and it is joyfully performed.*"

bhaktyā tv ananyayā śakya
aham evaṁ-vidho 'rjuna
jñātuṁ draṣṭuṁ ca tattvena
praveṣṭuṁ ca paran-tapa

(*Bhagavad-gītā* 11.54)

Translation: *"My dear Arjuna, only by undivided devotional service can I be understood as I am, standing before you, and can thus be seen directly. Only in this way can you enter into the mysteries of My understanding."*

Thus the direct experience and realization of God is the most clinching proof for the existence of God.

People say, "Show me God," but do they have the eyes to see God? Are they qualified?

What is the power of our eyes to see? In the dark we cannot even see our own hands in front of our eyes. So, one must try to develop spiritual vision by following an authorized spiritual process. Then one can actually be qualified.

God is not obliged to answer the challenges of any foolish, arrogant atheist. Once a well-known atheist said: "If there is a God in existence, He should prove it by killing me this very instant. If I continue to live after this challenge, then He does NOT exist." He did not die at that instant but he certainly did die some years later. God, of course, exists, and will do so eternally.

2.3. WRONG CONCEPTIONS OF GOD

As we have previously mentioned, many people today deny the very existence of God. Among the people who believe that God exists, there is much confusion.

Some of the wrong ideas about God are:

- God is light
- God is force
- God is void
- Everyone is God
- There are many Gods

- **God is dead**

So let us try to understand what "God" really is.

2.4. DEFINITION OF GOD

One may define God in many ways:

I) Source of Everything

Everything has a source. But God is He who is the source of everything. He is the cause of all the causes. He has no cause beyond Himself.

God is not only the origin of everything, but He is also the maintainer and destroyer.

(GOD – Generator, Operator, Destroyer)

God is the perfect, complete, whole and even though everything emanates from Him, He remains the same perfect complete, perfect whole. He does not diminish. The *Śrī Īśopaniṣad* declares:

oṁ pūrṇam adaḥ pūrṇam idaṁ
pūrṇāt pūrṇam udacyate
pūrṇasya pūrṇam ādāya
pūrṇam evāvaśiṣyate
(*Śrī Īśopaniṣad* Invocation)

Translation: "*The personality of Godhead is perfect and complete, and because He is completely perfect, all emanations from Him, such as this phenomenal world, are perfectly equipped as complete wholes. Whatever is produced of the Compete Whole is also complete in itself. Because He is the Complete Whole, even though so many complete units emanate from Him, He remains the complete balance.*"

II) Supreme Controller

He controls everything fully, everywhere and at all times.

He is **omniscient** (all – knowing) **Omnipotent** (all – powerful) **Omnipresent** (all – pervading)

We are all tiny, imitation controllers.

III) Supreme Proprietor

Everything belongs to Him, since everything comes from Him and is fully controlled by Him. We are false proprietors. Nothing actually belongs to us.

IV) Supreme Enjoyer

We can only enjoy something that belongs to us. Since everything belongs to God. He is the Supreme and indeed, only Enjoyer.

V) Possesses all opulences

"The word "bhaga" means opulences and "vān" means one who possesses. This is how the sage Parāśara Muni has defined the term "Bhagavān" in the *Viṣṇu Purāṇa*:

aiśvaryasya samagrasya
vīryasya yaśasaḥ śriyaḥ
jñāna-vairāgyayoś caiva
saṇṇāṁ bhaga itiṅgana

(*Viṣṇu Purāṇa* 6.5.47)

Translation: "*Full wealth, strength, fame, beauty, knowledge and renunciation – these are six opulences of the Supreme Personality of Godhead." An ordinary human may possess one or more of these opulences but in insignificant measure. God is He who possesses these opulences unlimitedly.*

All the above definitions define some particular transcendental feature or quality of God. There are innumerable such definitions possible.

Without satisfying these criteria, one cannot be considered God.

2.5. WHO IS GOD?

Śrī Kṛṣṇa is the Supreme Personality of Godhead. Why do we say this?

We say this because He fulfills all the criteria mentioned earlier, and the *Bhagavad-gītā* and other Vedic scriptures bear ample testimony to this.

Given below is just a small sample of vast scriptural evidence available in this regard:

I) Kṛṣṇa is the source of Everything

Not a blade of grass moves without His consent. Kṛṣṇa is the origin of everything. He declares:

ahaṁ sarvasya prabhavo
mattaḥ sarvaṁ pravartate
iti matvā bhajante māṁ
budhā bhāva-samanvitāḥ

(*Bhagavad-gītā* 10.8)

Translation: *"I am the source of all spiritual and material worlds. Everything emanates from Me. The wise who perfectly know this engage in My devotional service and worship Me with all their hearts."*

Furthermore, Brahmā, the secondary creator, says in *Brahma-saṁhitā*:

īśvaraḥ paramaḥ kṛṣṇaḥ
sac-cid-ānanda-vigrahaḥ
anādir ādir govindaḥ
sarva-kāraṇa-kāraṇam

(*Brahma-saṁhitā* Text 1)

Translation: *"Kṛṣṇa who is known as Govinda is the Supreme Godhead. He has an eternal blissful spiritual body. He is the origin of all. He has no other origin and He is the prime cause of all causes."*

II) Kṛṣṇa is the Supreme Controller

Everybody is helplessly controlled by material nature. All living being come into existence, play their parts and are inexorably annihilated. But Kṛṣṇa is the controller of material nature itself. The Lord says in *Bhagavad-gītā*:

mayādhyakṣeṇa prakṛtiḥ
sūyate sa-carācaram
hetunānena kaunteya
jagad viparivartate
(*Bhagavad-gītā* 9.10)

Translation: "*This material nature, which is one of My energies, is working under My direction, O son of Kuntī, producing all moving and nonmoving beings. Under its rule this manifestation is created and annihilated again and again.*"

III) Kṛṣṇa is the Supreme Proprietor of Everything

Everything belongs to Him and is meant for His enjoyment. We have nothing of our own, yet when we offer Kṛṣṇa, whatever is under our care, with love and devotion, He is pleased. We can see that when a child offers to his father a present bought out of his pocket money, the father is very pleased with the child because of the love shown by him. Kṛṣṇa describes in the *Bhagavad-gītā* the peace formula by which everyone can be happy and peaceful if they simply accept the proprietorship of Kṛṣṇa.

bhoktāraṁ yajña-tapasāṁ
sarva-loka-maheśvaram
suhṛdaṁ sarva-bhūtānāṁ
jñātvā māṁ śāntim ṛcchati
(*Bhagavad-gītā* 5.29)

Translation: "*A person in full consciousness of Me, knowing Me to be the ultimate beneficiary of all sacrifices and austerities, the Supreme Lord of all planets and demigods, and the benefactor and well-wisher of all living entities, attains peace from the pangs of material miseries.*"

IV) Kṛṣṇa is the Supreme Enjoyer

All work should be done as an offering to the Supreme Personality of Godhead since He is the Supreme bestower and enjoyer of all fruits. All sacrifices (*yajñas*) are meant to satisfy Him only. If Kṛṣṇa is pleased, everybody is pleased with our offering. Therefore He clearly states in the *Bhagavad-gītā* that it is He who is worshipped through all the various *yajñas*.

ahaṁ hi sarva-yajñānāṁ
bhoktā ca prabhur eva ca
na tu mām abhijānanti
tattvenātaś cyavanti te
(*Bhagavad-gītā* 9.24)

Translation: *"I am the only enjoyer and master of sacrifices. Therefore, those who do not recognize My true transcendental nature fall down."*

V) Kṛṣṇa is the Father of all

At the time of creation, Kṛṣṇa impregnates the material nature, and the living entities take birth in various forms according to their past deeds. Therefore, He is the father of all and we are His parts and parcels. This is confirmed by Lord Kṛṣṇa in the following verse:

sarva-yoniṣu kaunteya
mūrtayaḥ sambhavanti yāḥ
tāsāṁ brahma mahad yonir
ahaṁ bīja-pradaḥ pitā
(*Bhagavad-gītā* 14.4)

Translation: *"It should be understood that all species of life, O son of Kunti, are made possible by birth in this material nature, and that I am the seed giving father."*

VI) Kṛṣṇa is the Supreme Knower

Kṛṣṇa is all-knowing (omniscient). We have limited knowledge about ourselves and about material nature. But Kṛṣṇa knows everything whether in the past, present or future.Nothing is hidden from Him and there are no surprises for Him. Therefore He says:

vedāhaṁ samatītāni
vartamānāni cārjuna
bhaviṣyāṇi ca bhūtāni
māṁ tu veda na kaścana
(*Bhagavad-gītā* 7.26)

Translation: "*O Arjuna, as the Supreme Personality of Godhead, I know everything that has happened in the past, all that is happening in the present, and all things that are yet to come. I also know all living entities; but Me no one knows.*"

VII) Kṛṣṇa is The Supreme Absolute Truth

There is nothing higher than or equal to Kṛṣṇa. He is all pervading by His various energies and He is excellent in all respects. The Lord says:

mattaḥ parataraṁ nānyat
kiñcid asti dhanañ-jaya
mayi sarvam idaṁ protaṁ
sūtre maṇi-gaṇā iva
(*Bhagavad-gītā* 7.7)

Translation: "*O conqueror of wealth, there is no truth superior to Me. Everything rests upon Me, as pearls are strung on a thread.*"

VIII) All great sages declare Kṛṣṇa to be God

Arjuna declares to Kṛṣṇa in the *Bhagavad-gītā*:

arjuna uvāca

paraṁ brahma paraṁ dhāma
pavitraṁ paramaṁ bhavān
puruṣaṁ śāśvataṁ divyam
ādi-devam ajaṁ vibhum

āhus tvām ṛṣayaḥ sarve
devarṣir nāradas tathā
asito devalo vyāsaḥ
svayaṁ caiva bravīṣi me

(*Bhagavad-gītā* 10.12-13)

Translation: "*Arjuna said: You are the Supreme Personality of Godhead, the ultimate abode, the purest, the Absolute Truth. You are the eternal, transcendental, original person, the unborn, the greatest. All the great sages such as , Nārada, Asita, Devala and Vyāsa confirm this truth about You, and now You Yourself are declaring it to me.*"

Thus when we state that Kṛṣṇa is God, it is not out of some sentiment or personal bias but because of *śabda-pramāṇa* – the evidence of the scriptures.

2.6. THE EXPANSIONS OF GOD

Since Kṛṣṇa, the Supreme Personality of Godhead, is unlimited and is the complete perfect whole, He can expand Himself unlimitedly into any number of expansions without, in any way, diminishing Himself. He remains the complete whole as before.

Among the unlimited expansions of Kṛṣṇa, are innumerable ones that are equal to Him but possessing variegated forms, like Rāma, Narasiṁha, Nārāyaṇa, etc. These latter expansions are the same as the original Kṛṣṇa, but the only difference is of form and mood. They are all God.

The one Supreme Lord Kṛṣṇa manifests Himself in many forms same as, and equal to Himself. Therefore, we should consider all of Them to be simultaneously one and different from Kṛṣṇa, who is Their origin.

And the wonder is that even though Kṛṣṇa expands Himself into innumerable equals of Himself He remains the same Supreme Personality of Godhead.

This is spiritual mathematics : One minus one equals one!

This is a very important theological concept.

In the *Brahma-saṁhitā*, Brahma explains that: Kṛṣṇa is like the original candle that lights up many other candles. In other words,

He is the original source and fountain head of all other forms of the Lord.

This is also substantiated in the great scripture, the *Śrīmad-Bhāgavatam*:

ete cāṁṣa-kalāḥ puṁsaḥ
kṛṣṇas tu bhagavān svayam
indrāri-vyākulaṁ lokaṁ
mṛḍayanti yuge yuge
(*Śrīmad-Bhāgavatam* 1.3.28)

Translation: "*All of the above-mentioned incarnations are either plenary portions or portions of the plenary portions of the Lord, but Lord Śrī Kṛṣṇa is the original Personality of Godhead. All of them appear on planets whenever there is a disturbance created by the atheists. The Lord incarnates to protect the theists.*"

All these expansions are simply to help the original Supreme Personality of Godhead, Kṛṣṇa, enjoy different variegated tastes ('*rasas*') of love with His devotees.

All these wonderful spiritual forms of God reside eternally along with Their devotees in the Spiritual World, the Kingdom of God, called Vaikuṇṭha, which is far beyond the material universe. We will learn more about this in the theme 'Material nature (*Prakṛti*) and Time (*Kāla*)'.

LORD KṚṢṆA HAS TEN PRIMARY INCARNATIONS. STARTING FROM THE UPPER LEFT HAND CORNER TO RIGHT, THESE ARE:
1) MATSYA 2) KURMA 3) VARAHA 4) NRSIMHADEVA 5) VAMANADEVA 6) PARASHURAMA 7) RAMACHANDRA 8) BALARAMA 9) BUDDHA & 10) KALKI

2.7. THE DESCENT OF GOD

From time to time, the various forms of the Lord discussed above descend from Vaikuṇṭha into this material world. Then They are called "*Avatāras*" ("those who descend") or incarnations.

We should know these *Avatāras* to be fully spiritual and the Supreme Lord Himself. Ignorant people, however, often mistake Them for ordinary beings of this world because these *Avatāras* act, speak and live as if They were a part of this world.

The 'birth' and activities of these *Avatāras* in this world are called *līlās* or pastimes or sports, performed by Them according to Their own sweet will. We should not compare Their 'birth' and activities to ours. In the *Bhagavad-gītā*, Lord Kṛṣṇa explains:

janma karma ca me divyam
evaṁ yo vetti tattvataḥ
tyaktvā dehaṁ punar janma
naiti mām eti so 'rjuna

(*Bhagavad-gītā* 4.9)

Translation: "*One who knows the transcendental nature of My appearance and activities does not, upon leaving the body, take his birth again in this material world, but attains My eternal abode, O Arjuna.*"

Each *Avatāra* has a particular mission and form which is described in the scriptures.

However, in general, the *Avatāras* come for the following purposes:

A) To establish '***dharma***' and give knowledge of God and His activities

B) To protect the devotees and saintly persons, and

C) To destroy the miscreants who are mischievous and cause disruption in the peaceful and orderly functioning of the world.

As Lord Kṛṣṇa declares in the *Bhagavad-gītā*:

paritrāṇāya sādhūnāṁ
vināśāya ca duṣkṛtām
dharma-saṁsthāpanārthāya
sambhavāmi yuge yuge
(*Bhagavad-gītā* 4.8)

Translation: *"To deliver the pious and to annihilate the miscreants, as well as to reestablish the principles of religion, I Myself appear, millennium after millennium."*

But the most important reason for the descent of God into this world is to give pleasure to His devotees, and to attract the minds of the people of this world towards Him, by performing many sweet wonderful pastimes.

In other words, to give the nectar of Kṛṣṇa Consciousness or Love of God to everyone.

2.8. SYMPTOMS OF AN AVATĀRA

We find many unscrupulous people claiming to be an *Avatāra* of God and they cheat many gullible, innocent people, who are ignorant about spiritual truths. This is causing havoc in the society. Therefore, there must be a clear understanding of how one can recognize an *Avatāra*. Given below are the conditions that must be fulfilled. Otherwise, one should consider that person simply as a cheater.

I) He must be predicted in the scripture. (E.g. Lord Kalki, who will appear at the end of Kali Yuga).

II) He must display His Universal form (*Virāṭ-rūpa*). (As Lord Kṛṣṇa did to Arjuna).

III) He must perform extraordinary activities impossible for others to

perform. (As Lord Kṛṣṇa did by lifting the Govardhana Hill).

IV) He must have a unique message and mission. (E.g. Lord Caitanya came to establish Yuga-Dharma for Kali Yuga, *Hāriṇam-saṅkīrtan*).

V) He must have certain special marks and features on His body, as per the revealed scriptures. (E.g. On His palms and soles).

Lord Kṛṣṇa personally appeared about 5000 Years ago and Śrī Caitanya Mahāprabhu about 500 years ago.

The next *Avatāra* as per indications in the scripture will be Kalki *Avatāra*,– but that will happen more than 4 lakh years from now, at the end of Kali-yuga. There is no scheduled incarnation before that. Hence all those who claim to be *Avatāra* in the present day must be clearly understood to be imposters and cheaters.

2.9. ONE GOD OR MANY GODS?

One of the most common misconceptions, especially among Hindus, is that of pantheism i.e. the belief that there are many Gods. This is not true.

* **God (with a capital 'G') is one.**

There are, however, many Gods (with small 'g') called demigods, who are not in the category of God, but they represent God and reflect a tiny portion of His power.

The various expansions of God are referred to earlier (see under "Expansions of God") all fall under the 'capital G' God category. They are all God - one Supreme Person appearing as many Supreme Persons. These forms are many and varied, yet they are still one and the same Supreme Personality of Godhead.

As opposed to this, various personalities like Brahmā, Śiva, Indra, Ganesh, Durgā, Agni, Sūrya and so on, fall in the 'small-g', God category. That is they are demigods.

These two categories should not be equated.

- **Lord Kṛṣṇa and the other personalities in the 'God' are always Supreme and Independent, whereas the demigods are always subordinate and dependant.**
- **The demigods have no independent authority or power. This power is granted to them by Lord Kṛṣṇa for executing His purpose within this world. Hence, the demigods should never be considered 'God'.**
- **Lord Kṛṣṇa is actually the origin of all the demigods, as He declares in *Bhagavad-gītā*:**

na me viduḥ sura-gaṇāḥ
prabhavaṁ na maharṣayaḥ
aham ādir hi devānāṁ
maharṣīṇāṁ ca sarvaśaḥ
(***Bhagavad-gītā*** 10.2)

Translation: *"Neither the hosts of demigods nor the great sages know My origin or opulences, for, in every respect, I am the source of demigods and sages."*

- **The demigods are empowered living entities in charge of various administrative responsibilities for creation, maintenance and annihilation of the universe.** They are like ministers in a Government handling the affairs of a particular ministry. They remain in their posts as long as they enjoy the confidence of the Prime Minister (Kṛṣṇa). There are as many as 33 crores demigods.
- **Each universe has its own set of demigods.** Thus there are millions of Brahmās, Indras, Sūryas, in the creation. They perform their duties in accordance with the instructions of the Supreme Lord.

Just to give an idea, Some of the principal demigods along with their duties are given below:

DEMIGOD	FUNCTIONS
BRAHMĀ	Creation of the universe
ŚIVA	Destruction of the universe
INDRA	King of the demigods and in charge of rain and thunder
VARUṆA	In charge of all water bodies like oceans, rivers, lakes
SŪRYA	Provides heat and light
GANESHA	Removes obstacles from one's path
VĀYU	In charge of wind
KUVERA	Treasurer of the demigods
YAMARĀJA	God of death

- **These demigods reside in the higher planetary systems.** There they enjoy heavenly pleasures and a long life span. It is explained that the life span of Brahma, is 100 years which is equivalent to 311 trillion and 40 million earth years.
- **The demigods are devotees of the Lord and are the Lord's representatives in the universe.** The Supreme Lord is very merciful to them and He comes to their rescue whenever the demons threaten to annihilate them.

*** What should be one's attitude towards the demigods?**

Just as a representative of the Government is given due respect by the citizens, we should be respectful to the demigods. However, knowing

that Kṛṣṇa is the Supreme Lord, we need not worship the demigods separately for any material benefit. Whatever be our desires, whether for spiritual gain or material profit, we can directly approach Kṛṣṇa for their fulfillment. It is of course best to approach Kṛṣṇa exclusively for devotional service or *Bhakti.*

Although the demigods possess enormous powers, yet they also have to undergo birth and death. Hence they are not able to give the benediction of liberation. It is only Mukunda, "giver of liberation" (Kṛṣṇa) who is able to award this. Therefore, those who want the highest benefit in life always approach Kṛṣṇa and serve Him with resolute determination.

Kṛṣṇa says in the *Bhagavad-gītā* (7.20 and 7.23):

kāmais tais tair hṛta-jñānāḥ
prapadyante 'nya-devatāḥ
taṁ taṁ niyamam āsthāya
prakṛtyā niyatāḥ svayā
(*Bhagavad-gītā* 7.20)

Translation: "*Those whose intelligence has been stolen by material desires surrender unto demigods and follow the particular rules and regulations of worship according to their own natures.*"

antavat tu phalaṁ teṣāṁ
tad bhavaty alpa-medhasām
devān deva-yajo yānti
mad-bhaktā yānti mām api
(*Bhagavad-gītā* 7.23)

Translation: "*Men of small Intelligence worship the demigods, and their fruits are limited and temporary. Those who worship demigods go to the planets of the demigods, but My devotees ultimately reach My Supreme Planet.*"

For those who say that worship of the demigods is the same as worship of Kṛṣṇa, Kṛṣṇa replies that worship of the demigods is not the proper way to worship Him:

ye 'py anya-devatā-bhaktā
yajante śraddhayānvitāḥ
te 'pi mām eva kaunteya
yajanty avidhi-pūrvakam
(*Bhagavad-gītā* 9.23)

Translation: "*Those who are devotees of other Gods and who worship them with faith actually worship only Me, O son of Kunti, but they do so in a wrong way.*"

Furthermore, worshippers of Kṛṣṇa and those of the demigods and others, attain different destinations, so how can all such worship be one and the same?

yānti deva-vratā devān
pitṝn yānti pitṛ-vratāḥ
bhūtāni yānti bhūtejyā
yānti mad-yājino 'pi mām

(*Bhagavad-gītā* 9.25)

Translation: *"Those who worship the demigods will take birth among the demigods; those who worship the ancestors go to the ancestors; those who worship ghosts and spirits will take birth among such beings; and those who worship Me will live with Me."*

Therefore, while we should offer respect to the demigods, our worship, love and service should be offered directly to the Supreme Personality of Godhead, Śrī Kṛṣṇa.

2.10. IS KṚṢṆA A HINDU GOD?

No. God is God. God does not belong to this community or that. God is for everyone. He is not the monopoly of any particular class or group of people. So Kṛṣṇa is God for all, not just for Hindus or even all human beings, but for all species of life (as He declares in *Bhagavad-gītā* 14.4).

The same One God is known by different names in different languages in different cultures and lands at different times. 'Water' may be called as "jala" or "pānī" or "neeru" but it is still water; similarly with God.

The word "Allah" in Arabic means "all-powerful." The word "Jehovah" or "Yahweh" in Hebrew (from the Bible) means the greatest.

The word "Rāma" in Sanskrit means "all pleasing". The word "Kṛṣṇa" in Sanskrit means "all attractive". These different names refer to the same Supreme Personality of Godhead who possesses all opulences in full. Where is the contradiction?

2.11. KṚṢṆA IS THE HIGHEST CONCEPTION OF GOD

Kṛṣṇa means "all-attractive". Thus this name encompasses all other names and conceptions of God, and is the most intimate name. The Supreme Personality of Godhead as Lord Śrī Kṛṣṇa is revealed to us in the *Śrīmad- Bhāgavatam.* **He is described as possessing a body made of *sat-cit-ānanda* (eternity, bliss and knowledge). His beautiful complexion is dark blue like that of a new monsoon cloud. He is decorated with a peacock feather on His head and garlanded with Vaijayantī mālā. The sound of His flute is so melodious that anyone who hears it becomes enchanted. The peacocks immediately go mad, while all animals, trees and plants stand still and listen to the transcendental sound of the flute with great attention. Even the wives of the denizens of heaven become perturbed. The cows become charmed and immediately spread their long ears just to catch the liquid nectar of the flute. The *gopīs* of Vṛndāvana forget everything and simply run towards Kṛṣṇa. Thus Kṛṣṇa eternally enjoys loving pastimes with His devotees in His abode of Goloka.**

These same transcendental *līlās* were manifest on this earth planet when Kṛṣṇa descended along with His eternal companions and His abode in the holy land of Vraja (Vṛndāvana).

Kṛṣṇa is the reservoir of all pleasure and transcendental loving exchanges with His devotees is His only occupation. **This is the highest conception of God.**

2.12. WHY DIFFERENT RELIGIONS?

The question may be asked that if God is one, then why are there so many different religions?

The answer is that although God is one, when He appears, either directly or through His representatives (the saintly persons and

prophets), to disseminate knowledge about Himself, He presents this knowledge differently according to the time, place, circumstance and condition of His audience. Thus, there appears to be many religions. Actually, all bona fide religions are paths leading to God. The basic tenets or essential messages in all these religions are the same, namely,

- **This world is a place of suffering.**
- **Live a pure life, do not sin.**
- **Obey the laws or instructions of God**
- **Surrender to God, serve Him and love Him and so on.**

For example, all bona fide religions say God is one.

In the Bible, the one God is called Jehovah and Jesus, the "son of God" calls Him "Our father who art in Heaven". In the Quran, Prophet Mohammed says that there is only one God-Allah. In the *Bhagavad-gītā*, Lord Kṛṣṇa also declares that He Himself is the One Supreme Lord.

Yet there are differences, both in respect of their teachings and their conception of God. Just as there are different steps in a ladder, different religions occupy different levels in terms of their understanding of The Absolute Truth.

2.13. WHICH IS THE HIGHEST RELIGION?

- We have seen earlier that the Vedic scripture gives us the highest conception of God - Kṛṣṇa. The wonderful names, forms, associates, messages, abode, and paraphernalia of the Supreme Lord are described in great detail. This degree of detail is not found in any other scripture.
- For example, both the Quran and Bible only mention the Kingdom of God ("Heaven" or "paradise") but in the Vedic scripture we will find very elaborate descriptions down to minute details.

■ Similarly, although others scriptures speak at length about the qualities and messages of the Lord, they do not properly describe what He really looks like. In contrast, the Vedic scriptures contain vast and extremely detailed, authentic, sweet and poetic descriptions of the beautiful forms of the Lord.

■ The Vedic scriptures are like a large dictionary and the other scriptures are like pocket dictionaries. Both are bona fide, but the large dictionary contains much deeper and detailed information.

■ A professor teaching postgraduate students may also go and teach the same subject to high school students but he cannot teach exactly the same lesson. He has to simplify and condense the knowledge to make it understandable to the younger audience.

- Similarly, many of the Vedic scriptures were meant for sages who had pure minds and conduct, whose senses were controlled, and intelligence sharp and who were learned, austere and renounced. Hence, we find highly philosophical and deep discussions on subjects like ontology, theology, cosmology and so on.
- Even those of the Vedic scriptures that were intended for the common man presumed a certain high degree of spiritual culture, faith and discipline. On the other hand, the more recent religions were often directed when spoken by the prophets, to a certain class of people and in an environment, where the topmost spiritual knowledge had to be presented in a very simplified, summarized form that would be relevant and palatable to the audience.
- The Vedic scriptures teach the principle of *Sanātana-dharma,* the Eternal Religion for Man. It is thus the most ancient, original and highest religion of all.

2.14. TRUE RELIGION

The *Śrīmad-Bhāgavatam* declares :

sa vai puṁsāṁ paro dharmo
yato bhaktir adhokṣaje
ahaituky apratihatā
yayātmā suprasīdati
(*Śrīmad-Bhāgavatam* 1.2.6)

Translation: "*The Supreme occupation (dharma) for all humanity is that by which men can attain to loving devotional service unto the transcendental Lord. Such devotional service must be unmotivated and uninterrupted to completely satisfy the self.*"

This is the Standard for true religion – the extent to which one develops pure Love of God, regardless of what that religion may be called.

Hinduism, Islam, Christianity and so on are religious faiths, but true RELIGION is Love of God. This goes beyond narrow barriers of religious faiths.

The Vedic *Sanātana-dharma*, through the Vedic scriptures, facilitates in the most favorable way the development of love of God because of the super-excellent descriptions and conceptions of God contained therein, and the many sublime examples of great saintly lovers of God.

2.15. IS GOD A PERSON?

Is God a Person? Does He have form? Is He originally formless? This has been a debated topic for centuries.

The answer is that God is actually a Person - He is called "*ādi-pūruṣa*" i.e. the Original Person.

Being the Supreme all-attractive person, He naturally has a most beautiful form. And yet He also has a formless aspect just like the Sun has a form (the Sun-globe) and simultaneously also a formless aspect (the Sun rays).

This is called "*acintya-bhedābheda tattva*", the principle of inconceivable simultaneous oneness and difference. This has been explained very nicely by Śrī Caitanya Mahāprabhu.

It is explained in the Vedic literatures that the Absolute Truth has three aspects:

1) His personal feature, as Bhagavān, the source of everything and full of eternity, knowledge and bliss, who is known as 'Śrī Kṛṣṇa', the son of Nanda Mahārāja, the lover of the *gopīs* and the Lord of Dvārakā.

2) His expansion as Paramātmā, the Supersoul, the localized aspect, who is in the heart of all living entities. He witnesses their activities and guides them towards their supreme destination.

3) The Impersonal Brahman, which is simply the effulgence (halo) of the spiritual body of Kṛṣṇa. This is the formless aspect of God upon which the *yogis*, who desire to merge into God meditate.

This is confirmed in *Śrīmad-Bhāgavatam* by Sūta Gosvāmī:

vadanti tat tattva-vidas
tattvaṁ yaj jñānam advayam
brahmeti paramātmeti
bhagavān iti śabdyate
(*Śrīmad-Bhāgavatam* 1.2.11)

Translation: *"Learned transcendentalists who know the Absolute Truth call this nondual substance Brahman, Paramātmā or Bhagavān."*

The three aspects of the Supreme Truth exists simultaneously and there is no conflict between Them. However the personal aspect that is Bhagavān is the highest realization of the Absolute Truth. This can be explained with the help of an example.

The sun has three aspects, namely, sunshine, the sun planet and the sun God.

SUNSHINE
(BRAHMAN)

SUNGLOBE
(PARAMĀTMĀ)

SUN GOD SŪRYADEVA (BHAGAVĀN)

The three are existing simultaneously and are in one sense similar. Yet the Sunshine originates from the sun planet which is regulated by the sun god who resides within. The sun god (Sūryadeva) may not be visible to us from here. But if we go to the sun planet, we can see the sun god, who is the controller of the sunshine.

In the same way, the existence of the impersonal Brahman depends upon the Personality of Godhead even though the Personality of Godhead is not visible to us from here.

- **Therefore, the conception of the impersonal Brahman is the preliminary understanding of the Absolute Truth.**
- **When one advances further, one understands the localized aspect, Paramātmā who is situated in everyone's heart.**
- **Finally, one comes to the understanding of Bhagavān, the Supreme Personality of Godhead, Kṛṣṇa, who is the source of both Brahman and Paramātmā.**

Just as knowing the Sun only to the extent of the sun rays and not beyond is not wrong, but simply incomplete, similarly knowing the Absolute Truth as Impersonal is not wrong but is an incomplete understanding.

One who understands the Absolute Truth only as Brahman cannot understand the other aspects of the Truth. But one who understands Bhagavān, also understands Paramātmā and Brahman. Because his understanding is the highest, it includes the understanding of the lower two aspects of the Absolute Truth. In other words, his understanding is complete and perfect.

Thus one must know the Absolute Truth to be essentially the Supreme Person who has a secondary impersonal feature also. In the *Bhagavad -gītā* Kṛṣṇa says,

brahmaṇo hi pratiṣṭhāham
amṛtasyāvyayasya ca
śāśvatasya ca dharmasya
sukhasyaikāntikasya ca
(*Bhagavad-gītā* 14.27)

Translation: *"And I am the basis of the impersonal Brahman, which is immortal, imperishable and eternal and is the constitutional position of ultimate happiness."*

Kṛṣṇa admonishes those who think that He is originally without a form but assumes a form when adventing in this world. He declares in *Bhagavad-gītā*:

avyaktaṁ vyaktim āpannaṁ
manyante mām abuddhayaḥ
paraṁ bhāvam ajānanto
mamāvyayam anuttamam
(*Bhagavad-gītā* 7.24)

Translation: *"Unintelligent men, who do not know Me perfectly, think that I, the Supreme Personality of Godhead, Kṛṣṇa, was impersonal before and have now assumed this personality. Due to their small knowledge, they do not know My highest nature, which is imperishable and supreme."*

Kṛṣṇa, often says "mām", "mama" etc when referring to Himself as the Supreme Personality of Godhead. He says that we should become His devotees, offer our homage unto Him, chant His glories and surrender unto Him. He does not say that we should worship the impersonal Brahman.

Therefore Kṛṣṇa's form and activities are transcendental and not on the material plane. In spite of having a form Kṛṣṇa still remains higher than the highest, lighter then the lightest, heavier than the heaviest and so on.

When Kṛṣṇa was performing His pastimes (*līlās*) in Gokula, one demon by name of Tṛṇāvarta came there in the form a whirlwind.

He picked up baby Kṛṣṇa in his arms and took Him high over the clouds. At that time Kṛṣṇa became so heavy that the demon crashed to the ground and died. This incident shows that Kṛṣṇa is never limited by His form.

2.16. LOGIC TO ESTABLISH THAT GOD IS A PERSON

Those who follow the impersonalist philosophy say that,

- God is impersonal
- And thus He has no form
- They say that God is unlimited and if He were to have form that would limit Him. Therefore, He cannot have form.
- The truth however, is that to say that God cannot have form is to limit Him.
- If He is truly unlimited, then He must have everything - including form.
- We have form. So how can God, who is our source, not have form? How can the part have something that is not there in the whole?
- God is complete and whole. Therefore, He must have everything that His parts have and more.
- Air is formless; therefore, God must have formlessness as well. Only when He has both, can God be called complete. This is the principle of ***acintya-bhedābheda*** as we have seen earlier.

However, of the two attributes – form and formless - form is superior, or it is the origin of the latter. Therefore, ultimately God is a Person.

The impersonalists:

- Deny the form of the Lord as they only have experience of material forms.
- They speculate that God's form, when He descends on earth, must also be made of matter.
- Material forms have many limitations. On the other hand, by definition, God is unlimited. Therefore He cannot have a form.

This is their logic.

But a flaw in this logic is that they assume that God's form is material.

- **Kṛṣṇa is "*sac-cid-ānanda-vigraha*"-a pure spiritual form of eternity, knowledge and bliss.**
- **Since God's form is completely spiritual and unlimited, He can expand Himself unlimitedly and still remain the complete whole.**

As explained earlier, God is the supreme controller. Nothing can happen without His sanction. From our experience we can see that whenever there is a controller there has to be a personality. The government controls the life of the citizens which is in turn under the control of the Prime Minister. A power station may be controlled by a computer, but a software programmer controls the computer. In the same way, we can understand the controller behind this gigantic and complex material creation must also be a person.

3. SOUL

CHAPTER 3

SOUL

WHO AM I?
UNDERSTANDING THE SOUL
THE LOGIC OF REINCARNATION

3.1. WHO AM I?

■ This question has plagued philosophers from time immemorial. Since man is a "thinking animal", he is not simply satisfied by trying to fulfill his basic needs. He asks many questions about his surroundings, his planet, his universe and about the mystery of his own existence-the mystery of "Who am I?"

WHAT IS LIFE ?

WHAT IS CONSCIOUSNESS?

WHO AM I?

WHAT IS DEATH?

■ A person who wants to live life to its full has to first understand this basic question, "Who am I?", without which he remains like an animal only satisfied with eating, sleeping, mating and defending. He does not know the source of his problems nor how to solve them.

■ Modern science deals with this vital question in a very mechanistic manner, stating that man is nothing but a combination of certain material elements, the smallest parts of which are atoms or electrons, which constitute the origin of life.

■ According to modern science, life is the result of a series of transformations of non-living matter. This is the 'Theory of Evolution', first propounded in recent times by Charles Darwin. Atoms combined to form simple molecules, then by further combinations came more and more complex molecules and then suddenly, lo and behold!, life sprouted from there. The inert matter suddenly became living.

■ The simplest living organism was thus born. With continued evolution, more complex organisms were produced. As these organisms became better and better through further reproduction and adaptation, this evolution structure ultimately produced all forms of life that ever existed on earth, finally reaching its apex in man. And all this is believed to have been accomplished without intelligent direction.

■ Atheistic thinkers today are using this evolution theory to try to establish that, there is no need to believe in a Personal God. After all, life has simply evolved from chemicals by chance and simple physical laws operating over an immense span of time.

■ Hence, the modern scientific conception of the 'self' or 'I', is that we are simply a collection of atoms and molecules, and all our emotions, thought processes and so on, are simply certain physiological changes taking place within the body.

■ But, am I simply a bunch of atoms? Is this really life? Thankfully, some thoughtful scientists are not so convinced. Nobel Laureate Albert Szent –Gyorgyi commented, "In my search for life, I ended up with atoms and electrons which have no life at all, and somewhere along the line, life has run out through my fingers."

- And then, what is 'death'? The law defines death as the "absence of life". But no clear understanding exists today on the exact nature of life. How, then, would one define life? Life is simply distinguished by certain symptoms. Hence both "life" and "death" remain great puzzles.
- So let us try to address these issues.

3.2. WHAT IS LIFE?

To understand this, let us start with a simple illustration of a play, which is being watched by two entities,

- A man (living being), and
- A camera (non living being)

But still there is a distinct difference between the observers.

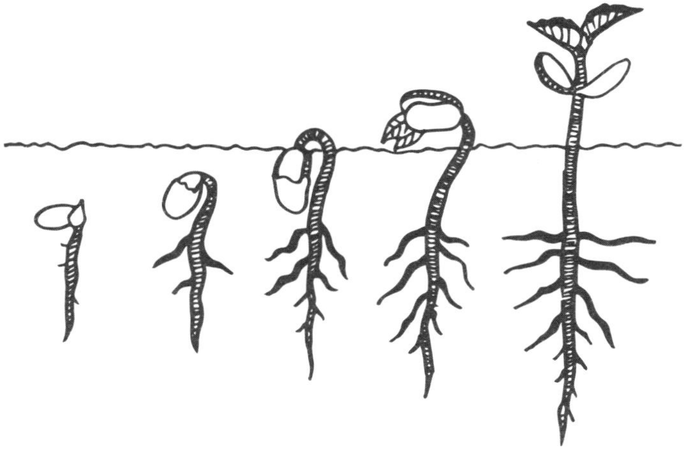

R.I.P.

So what is the difference between the (living) man and the (non-living) camera? It is consciousness.

In other words, life is consciousness.

3.3. WHAT IS CONSCIOUSNESS?

Consciousness means the awareness of being, i.e. "I am." The very fact that we are asking the question, "Who am I?" means that we are conscious living entities. On the other hand a non-living thing can never ask a question like this.

Consciousness also means the ability to think, feel and will, as illustrated in the above example.

It is consciousness that distinguishes the living from the dead. To make things more clear, let us note the difference in the consciousness of a living body and a dead body.

When the body is in the living condition, it responds to even slightest stimuli like, a pinch or feeling of heat or cold. On the other hand, a dead body does not react to a postmortem examination or even when it is thrown in fire or in a deep freezer.

Thus the difference between the living and the dead is the presence or absence of consciousness.

Since consciousness is what makes something alive, the question arises, **What is the source of this consciousness?**

3.4. WHAT IS THE SOURCE OF CONSCIOUSNESS?

As we have seen above, modern science believes that consciousness is produced merely by the interaction of molecules and chemicals.

However, given below are seven good reasons to believe otherwise - that the source of consciousness is distinct from the body.

I) Who sees and hears?

When I say, "I see" or "I hear", who is it that is actually seeing or hearing? Is it my eye that sees? Or my ear that hears? A dead body has eyes and ears but it does not see or hear. Why?

Is the perception of sight or hearing, in the brain or the nervous system of the body then? But a dead body has a brain and nervous system too, yet it does not see or hear. Why?

The answer is that, the perceiving is being done by something or someone distinct from the body.

II) Put back chemicals in a dead body and make it alive!

If chemicals are indeed the source of life or consciousness as the scientists say, then one can simply put the chemicals back in a dead body and make it alive again!

But this cannot be done because life does not come from matter but from some other source. Scientists have never been able to show or prove their claim by making dead things come to life.

It is our unfailing, common experience that life comes only from life, and not from dead matter or chemicals.

III) Common-sense understanding

When a person dies, the relatives lament, "oh! He has passed away". But, who has passed away? The person they love is still lying there.

The body has not gone anywhere. So who has gone away? **Obviously, something which is different from the body and which made the body appear 'alive' has gone away.**

IV) Intuitive understanding

We say, "My hand", "My body", and so on, not "I hand", or "I body", meaning thereby that my hand, body etc. are different from 'me', the owner of these things.

So who is that 'me' or 'I' who owns this body and who drives it?

V) Body changes but 'I' remains the same

At every moment from conception in the womb till death, our body is constantly changing. In his book, "The Human Brain", Prof. John Pfeiffer notes that, "Your body does not contain a single one of the molecules that it contained seven years ago...." That means every seven years our whole body changes. Yet, our sense of identity, or 'I' ness remains.

In other words the source of 'I' ness or consciousness, does not change with changes in the body. Therefore, it must be something different from and superior to the body.

VI) Out-of-Body Experiences (OBE)/ Near-Death-Experiences (NDE)

Evidence that the source of consciousness must be distinct from the body is also supported by research on Near-Death-Experiences (NDE). Sometimes, people on the verge of death have reported having extraordinary and baffling experiences that defy modern scientific understanding.

NDE includes out of body experiences (OBE) in which people report observing their physical body and events relating to it from a point outside of the body during severe illness or physical trauma resulting into unconsciousness.

A typical case might be a person who recovers from a heart attack or from a major traffic accident and reports that he observed from a point outside his body, the medical personal helping to revive him. By all medical standards, the patient should have been unconscious and in no position at all, to make such observations. In some of these cases the patients gave very detailed and accurate descriptions of the operating and medical procedures and what went on in the operation theatre.

Indeed the big question is who was observing the operation-taking place? The body was unconscious and lying on the table. Therefore, the real observer or the source of consciousness must have been distinct from the body.

A great deal of research work in NDEs has been done by professionals of good scientific standing. For example, Dr. Michel Sabom, Cardiologist at the Emory University Medical School in U.S.A. was quite skeptical at first but changed his mind after investigating NDEs thoroughly. He raised several fundamental questions and mused whether the source of consciousness could be separate from the physical body.

VII) Past-life memories

Over the years there have been many reports of memories of a previous life by people of different communities, religious faiths and nationalities throughout the world. Typically, such reports are made by children (only sometimes adults) and include detailed and accurate descriptions (and identification) of people, places and events of their previous life. This information should normally have been impossible for these people to know.

Many of these reports have been confirmed by rigorous and unbiased studies by professionals like Dr. Ian Stevenson of University of Virginia, U.S.A, who have taken great care to check the possibility of fraud and deception.

In one of his works, "Twenty Cases Suggestive of Reincarnation", Dr. Stevenson reports the case of Shukla, the daughter of a Bengali railway worker. When she was very young, she would cradle a pillow in her arms like a doll and call it by the name, Minu. She behaved as if Minu were her daughter, and also spoke of Minu's father and his two brothers. According to Shukla, they all lived in Bhatpara, and she insisted her parents take her there. Shukla's father investigated and learned that there had lived in Bhatpara a woman named Mana, who had died a few years before, leaving behind a baby daughter named Minu.

Shukla's father became convinced his daughter had previously lived as Mana. When Shukla was brought by her family to Bhatpara, she led them to the house where Mana had lived. Then, from a group of over thirty strangers, she picked out Mana's husband, mother-in-law, and brother- in-law as well as the girl Minu. These details and many others were extensively researched and corroborated.

In another report, "A Copy of Xenoglossy," Dr. Stevenson cites the case of an American woman living in Philadelphia who was regressed hypnotically and manifested the personality of a Swedish farmer. She spoke fluent Swedish, although she had no prior contact with Swedish in her life; natives Swedes confirmed her pronunciation to be fluent, even though many Swedish ovals sounds are extremely difficult for Americans to pronounce.

In India too, cases of people with memories of a previous life are in abundance. Some of these cases have received prominent coverage in the media.

The Vedic scriptures are also replete with histories of people with past -life memories and also descriptions of multiple lives of particular individuals.

For instance, in the *Śrīmad-Bhāgavatam*, the great sage Nārada Muni narrates to his disciple Vyāsadeva, the compiler of the *Vedas*, episodes from his previous life as the young son of a maidservant.

Another well-known history is that of Mahārāja Bharata (after whom this land is known as Bhārata varṣa), who became a deer in the next life, and in the birth thereafter, he was born in a family of *brāhmaṇas*. In his births as a deer and a *brāhmaṇa*, he clearly remembered his life as Mahārāja Bharata.

So what conclusions can we draw from these narrations, both present and ancient, Indian and Western?

Consider this: At death, the body, including the contents of the brain, is fully destroyed. What then is the connecting link between the previous life and the present one?

It must obviously be something that is different from the body, which is not destroyed when the previous body is destroyed, and which is transferred to the new body after the destruction of the previous body.

The studies of Dr. Stevenson and others give convincing evidence that there is a conscious self that is distinct from the body and that it can travel from one physical body to the next.

So if consciousness is distinct from the body, then what is actually the source of this consciousness? The *Bhagavad-gītā* gives the answer.

3.5. SOUL IS THE SOURCE OF CONSCIOUSNESS

In the *Bhagavad-gītā*, Lord Kṛṣṇa explains that the source of the consciousness is the spirit soul, the '*ātma*', which is eternal and spiritual.

We have seen above seven good reasons to believe that the source of consciousness is distinct from the body.

Now, we see the most conclusive and compelling reason, the statement of the *Bhagavad-gītā* that the spirit soul is the source of consciousness. *Bhagavad-gītā*, as we have seen earlier, is ***śabda pramāṇa***, i.e. infallible wisdom, free from defects, because it is the word of God. Therefore, it provides us with the most clear and authoritative answer to the mystery of consciousness.

In other words why do we accept that the soul exists and that it is source of consciousness? There are so many logical reasons but the ultimate answer is, because the *Bhagavad-gītā* says so.

Lord Kṛṣṇa explains in the *Bhagavad-gītā* that the eternal soul distributes consciousness throughout the body.

Consciousness is, thus, the symptom of the soul. Since the soul is eternal, its symptom i.e. consciousness is also eternal and imperishable.

avināśi tu tad viddhi
yena sarvam idaṁ tatam
vināśam avyayasyāsya
na kaścit kartum arhati

(*Bhagavad-gītā* 2.17)

Translation: "*That which pervades the entire body you should know to be indestructible. No one is able to destroy that imperishable soul.*"

Although the soul is located at one point, in the region of the heart, consciousness pervades the entire body just as sunshine pervades the entire universe even though the sun is located at one point.

eṣo 'ṇur ātmā cetasā veditavyo
yasmin prāṇaḥ pañcadhā saṁviveśa
prāṇaiś cittaṁ sarvam otaṁ prajānāṁ
yasmin viśuddhe vibhavaty eṣa ātmā

(*Muṇḍaka Upaniṣad* 3.1.9)

Translation: "*The soul is atomic in size and can be perceived by perfect intelligence. This atomic soul is floating in the five kinds of air [prāṇa, apāna, vyāna, samāna and udāna]. The soul is situated within the heart, and it spreads its influence all over the body of the embodied living entities. When the soul is purified from the contamination of the five kinds of material air, its spiritual influence is exhibited.*"

For those who still persist in asking, how they can understand that the soul exists, when they cannot see it, here is the answer: we can

understand the presence of the soul within the body, even though we cannot see it, by the presence of its symptom, namely, consciousness, just as we can understand the presence of the sun while seated in a room by presence of sunshine, or just as a doctor can diagnose the disease of a patient by simply studying the symptoms.

The fact that the soul cannot be seen with our eyes is not important. We have already seen in the Introduction section of this book that pratyakṣa pramāṇa is highly undependable and is not independently capable of leading us to perfect knowledge. So let us accept Lord Kṛṣṇa's statement in the *Bhagavad-gītā* and easily find true knowledge. **The answer to the question, "Who am I?", therefore is: "I am the eternal spirit soul. I am not the material body."**

3.6. SOME OTHER QUALITIES OF THE SOUL

Let us try to learn something more about the soul from the scriptures:

I) The soul is eternal

na jāyate mriyate vā kadācin
nāyaṁ bhūtvā bhavitā vā na bhūyaḥ
ajo nityaḥ śāśvato 'yaṁ purāṇo
na hanyate hanyamāne śarīre
(*Bhagavad-gītā* 2.20)

Translation: "*For the soul there is neither birth nor death at any time. He has not come into being, does not come into being, and will not come into being. He is unborn, eternal, ever existing and primeval. He is not slain when the body is slain.*"

II) The soul is imperishable

nainaṁ chindanti śastrāṇi
nainaṁ dahati pāvakaḥ
na cainaṁ kledayanty āpo
na śoṣayati mārutaḥ

(*Bhagavad-gītā* 2.23)

Translation: *"The soul can never be cut to pieces by any weapon, nor burned by fire, not moistened by water, nor withered by the wind."*

III) The soul is eternally an individual

The soul never loses its identity even after death or liberation.

na tv evāhaṁ jātu nāsaṁ
na tvaṁ neme janādhipāḥ
na caiva na bhaviṣyāmaḥ
sarve vayam ataḥ param

(*Bhagavad-gītā* 2.12)

Translation: *"Never was there a time when I did not exist, nor you, nor all these kings; nor in the future shall any of us cease to be."*

IV) The size of the soul

The soul is extremely tiny in size – it is said to be the dimension of 1/10,000 the tip of a hair!

bālāgra-śata-bhāgasya
śatadhā kalpitasya ca
bhāgo jīvaḥ sa vijñeyaḥ
sa cānantyāya kalpate

(*Śvetāśvatara Upaniṣad* 5.9)

Translation: *"When the upper point of the hair is divided into 100 parts* *and each of such part is further divided into 100 parts, each such part is the measurement of the dimension of the spirit soul."*

V) The soul is amazing

The tiny soul powers the small body of a germ as well as the huge body of an elephant. It is truly amazing!

āścarya-vat paśyati kaścid enam
āścarya-vad vadati tathaiva cānyaḥ
āścarya-vac cainam anyaḥ śṛṇoti
śrutvāpy enaṁ veda na caiva kaścit
(*Bhagavad-gītā* 2.29)

Translation: *"Some look on the soul as amazing, some describe him as amazing, and some hear of him as amazing, while others, even after hearing about him, cannot understand him at all."*

3.7. WHAT IS DEATH?

Having answered the question, "What is life?" (Answer: Life is the spirit soul, the '*ātmā*'), we are now in a position to answer the question: **"What is death?"**

The answer is very simple: **death is the departure of the spirit soul from the material body.** That's all.

The soul is the real person, the 'I' who resides within the body. And when the soul leaves, the body perishes.

Sometimes, a person lapses into coma or an unconscious state prior to death. This indicates that while nature is urging the soul to leave the body, the soul is struggling to remain there due to attachment. Finally, however, sooner or later, the soul will have to depart.

3.8. THE BODY IS ALWAYS DEAD

Surprising as it may sound, this is true. The body is simply dead matter. The body was always dead, it is now dead and it will remain so in the future. It is only the soul that is alive. Our understanding of death will be more complete when we understand this.

It is the presence of the soul within the body that makes the body appear alive and exhibit symptoms of consciousness.

Here is the good example to understand this point. The body is like a car and the soul is like a driver of the car. The car moves, produces sound and exhibits what appear to be symptoms of life to an ignorant eye. But actually the car, even though moving, is always dead. It is only because the driver is present within, can the car do all these things.

Similarly, it is only because the soul is present within the body, that the body can walk, talk, eat and so on. And all the while, the body remains dead.

The body is actually just a lump of flesh, bones, chemicals, and so on. The market value of all the chemicals that make up the body is only a few hundred rupees.

But we are willing to spend lakhs of rupees to preserve this body. Why? Because it is the soul that gives value to the body and when the soul leaves the body, the body is immediately disposed off by the relatives. The body ceases to have value any more. Then no amount of manipulation of chemicals and organs can revive the body, because the soul has already departed.

3.9. COMPARISON BETWEEN SPIRIT-SOUL AND MATTER

SPIRIT-SOUL (*ātmā*)	MATTER (material body)
SAT (Eternal)	*ASAT* (forms are ever-changing)
CIT (conscious, having knowledge)	*ACIT* (not conscious, full of ignorance)
ĀNANDA (blissful)	*NIRĀNANDA* (without bliss, prone to suffering)
HAS FORM	HAS TO BE GIVEN A FORM
HAS INDIVIDUALITY	HAS NO INDIVIDUALITY
BELONGS TO THE SPIRITUAL WORLD	BELONGS TO THE MATERIAL WORLD

3.10. TWO ENERGIES OF GOD

In the *Bhagavad-gītā* (7.4-5), Lord Kṛṣṇa speaks about His two energies in this world:

bhūmir āpo 'nalo vāyuḥ
khaṁ mano buddhir eva ca
ahaṅkāra itīyaṁ me
bhinnā prakṛtir aṣṭadhā
(*Bhagavad-gītā* 7.4)

Translation: "*Earth, water, fire, air, ether, mind, intelligence and false ego – all together these eight constitute My separated material energies.*"

apareyam itas tv anyāṁ
prakṛtiṁ viddhi me parām
jīva-bhūtāṁ mahā-bāho
yayedaṁ dhāryate jagat
(*Bhagavad-gītā* 7.5)

Translation: *"Besides these, O mighty-armed Arjuna, there is another, superior energy of Mine, which comprises the living entities who are exploiting the resources of this material, inferior nature."*

The material energy is called inferior energy and the spiritual energy (comprising the souls) is called superior energy.

The chart below outlines the information given in these two verses:

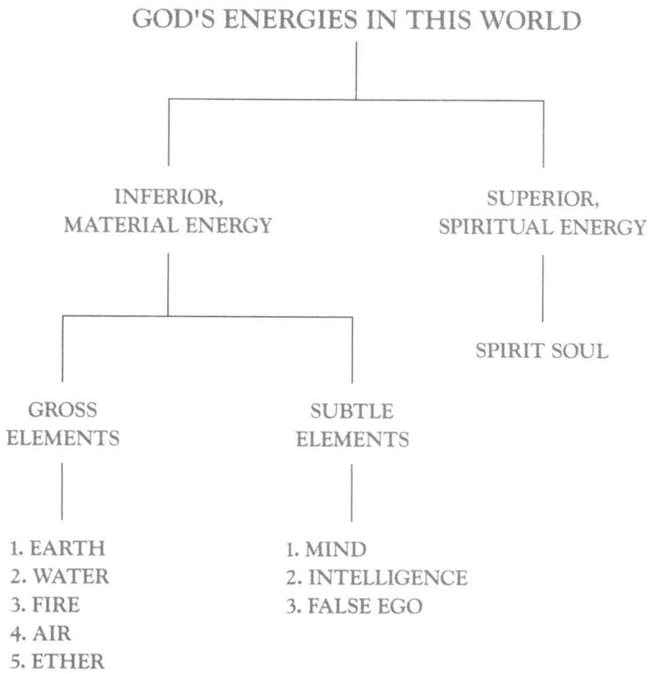

3.11. THE TWO BODIES

We have seen above that the material energy has 5 gross elements and 3 subtle elements.

Therefore the material body also, therefore, can be said to be composed of two bodies:

1. The gross body, and the other,
2. The subtle body

The gross body is, in ordinary terms, our physical body comprising earth (solid element), water (liquid element), fire (heat element), air (gas element) and ether (space element). Earth is the grossest element and ether is the most subtle.

The subtle body comprises mind, intelligence and false ego. These three elements cannot be directly perceived by any of our senses, although they can be experienced.

- The mind is the storehouse of desires and memories.
- Intelligence is the faculty of discrimination.
- False ego, the subtlest of all brings the eternal soul under illusion and makes it identify itself with the temporary material body.

The soul, of course, being non-material is superior to all the above eight elements. It is beyond the two bodies and is the proprietor of both. Lord Kṛṣṇa says in the *Bhagavad-gītā*:

indriyāṇi parāṇy āhur
indriyebhyaḥ paraṁ manaḥ
manasas tu parā buddhir
yo buddheḥ paratas tu saḥ
(*Bhagavad-gītā* 3.42)

Translation: *"The working senses are superior to dull matter; mind is* *higher than the senses; intelligence is still higher than the mind; and he (the soul) is even higher than the intelligence."*

3.12. CHARIOT OF THE BODY

CHARIOT	BODY
HORSES	SENSES
REINS	MIND
DRIVER	INTELLIGENCE
PASSENGER	SOUL

The Vedic literatures explain that the body-soul combination may be compared to be a chariot. Here is the comparison:

When the intelligence is pure, spiritual and strong, then it can control the mind, which in turn can control the senses just as a good driver controls the reins and thus the horses as well. The overall purpose of the soul-body arrangement can be fulfilled only if the senses are controlled.

When the intelligence is contaminated and weak, the mind and senses, which are full of material desires for enjoyment, carry away the chariot of the body in a very dangerous and uncontrolled way. Therefore the intelligence must be nourished and made resolute through spiritual knowledge.

3.13. THE CAGE POLISHING CIVILIZATION

Unfortunately, instead of pursuing spiritual knowledge, people run after the pleasures of this world. **It is very surprising that most of our life revolves around matter, and we forget the spirit soul, which is eternal. It is equally amazing that people accept the body to be permanent.** We all have sufficient experience that the happiness of the body is temporary and flickering. Still we are attached to it as if it is permanent. This is a recipe for misery.

It is explained that the body is like a cage and the soul like a bird within. If one simply polishes the cage but neglects to feed the bird, what will be the result?

There was once a lady who had a pet parrot who was kept in a golden cage. She cleaned and polished the cage everyday but neglected the parrot completely. Soon, being deprived of food and water, the parrot died.

Similarly our modern society is simply a cage polishing civilization which caters to the unlimited demands of the body but completely ignores the needs of the soul.

How, then, can there be peace and happiness in society?

3.14. THE SOUL IS ETERNALLY PART AND PARCEL OF GOD

The soul is an eternal fragmental portion of God's spiritual energy, and is thus eternally linked to God in a bond of service and devotion. Lord Kṛṣṇa says in *Bhagavad-gītā:*

mamaivāṁśo jīva-loke
jīva-bhūtaḥ sanātanaḥ
manaḥ-ṣaṣṭhānīndriyāṇi
prakṛti-sthāni karṣati
(*Bhagavad-gītā* 15.7)

Translation: *"The living entities in this conditioned world are My eternal fragmental parts. Due to conditioned life, they are struggling very hard with the six senses, which include the mind."*

- **The soul is the part and God is the whole. That is, the soul can never become God.**

- **We are not God, but we are God's. That is, we are God's property and therefore we should only be engaged in His service.**

"*Ahaṁ brahmāsmi*" means "I am spirit, not matter". The soul is Brahman (spirit) but God is Parabrahman (Supreme Spirit). Hence, "*ahaṁ brahmāsmi*" should never be taken to mean that "I am God".

- **Those who propagate the phrase "So'ham" (which means "I am He"), believe that God is impersonal and that we are that same Whole.**

- **But this is not true, we are like God in quality (i.e., we are both spiritual) but we are not the same in quantity. This is called the principle of *acintya-bhedābheda*-"inconceivable simultaneous oneness and difference."**

God is infinite and we are tiny, infinitesimal.

GOD	SPIRIT SOUL
Supreme Soul	Individual Soul
Infinite (*Vibhu*)	Infinitesimal (*Aṇu*)
Supremely Conscious	Individually Conscious
Eternally Master	Eternally Servant

The soul belongs to the Kingdom of God, the spiritual world, but it is now lost here in the material world. By reviving its original relationship with God, it can return home, back to Godhead.

3.15. WHAT HAPPENS TO THE SOUL AFTER DEATH?

Since the body is perishable and the soul is eternal, the question naturally arises: Where does the soul go after death?

Lord Kṛṣṇa answers that, the soul occupies another material body after leaving the previous one. This is reincarnation or transmigration. The soul accepts one body after another. In this way the cycle of birth and death goes on.

3.16. WHAT IS THE LOGIC BEHIND THE IDEA OF REINCARNATION?

Lord Kṛṣṇa explains in *Bhagavad-gītā* that reincarnation (or change of body) takes place even in this life.

From childhood, youth to old age, the soul moves through various bodies in one life. Similarly, at death the soul moves to another body.

dehino 'smin yathā dehe
kaumāraṁ yauvanaṁ jarā
tathā dehāntara-prāptir
dhīras tatra na muhyati
(**Bhagavad-gītā** 2.13)

Translation: *"As the embodied soul continuously passes, in this body, from boyhood to youth to old age, the soul similarly passes into another body at death. A sober person is not bewildered by such a change."*

Lord Kṛṣṇa explains that the material body is like a dress for the soul. Just as we change our clothes periodically and wear new ones, similarly, the soul discards the old body when it is no longer useful, and accepts a new one.

vāsāṁsi jīrṇāni yathā vihāya
navāni gṛhṇāti naro 'parāṇi
tathā śarīrāṇi vihāya jīrṇāny
anyāni saṁyāti navāni dehī
(**Bhagavad-gītā** 2.22)

Translation: *"As a person puts on new garments, giving up old ones, the soul similarly accepts new material bodies, giving up the old and useless ones."*

The body is also like a car or apartment and the soul is like a driver or resident. Just as we give up an old car to buy a new one, similarly the soul leaves the old body and accepts a new one. Why is one child born in a wealthy family and another in a poor family? Why someone is mentally retarded and someone gifted with a natural intelligence? Why is there such disparity from birth? This can be explained only if we understand that there is a previous life and that, the present birth has taken place in accordance with the activities (*Karma*) of the previous life. We will discuss more about this in the next section.

4. THE WHEEL OF SAṀSĀRA & THE LAW OF KARMA

Exposure
MAG.

CHAPTER 4

THE WHEEL OF SAṀSĀRA & THE LAW OF KARMA

4.1. REINCARNATION IS A LAW OF NATURE

■ We have seen in the previous section (section 3), that the eternal soul leaves the perishable body at the time of death and occupies a new body. This is reincarnation or transmigration.

■ The logic to establish that such a phenomenon takes place was also discussed. By practical evidence laid through past-life memories of various people, the logic for reincarnation was made stronger. And finally, the scriptural evidence (*śabda-pramāṇa*) cited makes it imperative for us to believe in reincarnation.

■ **Reincarnation therefore, is not just a 'Hindu' idea, as many people believe. It is a Law of Nature.**

■ Nature does not distinguish between caste, creed, religious faith, and so on.

■ Every living being in this creation has to undergo repeated birth and death.

■ Hindus, Muslims, Christians and others will all have to die and be re-born. Indians, Russians, Japanese and people of all nations will always have to be re-born.

■ So will all animals, birds and insects. No one can escape.

■ **Just as the 'Law of Gravity' acts on all the people, regardless of their caste, creed and so on, the 'Law of Transmigration', being a Law**

of Nature, acts on all.

■ It does not matter whether one knows about the law or not, or whether one believes it or not. The law will act-relentlessly, continuously, and unavoidably, life after life.

4.2. THE WHEEL OF SAṀSĀRA

'Saṁsāra' refers to this world of birth and death.

It is like a wheel because the soul has to repeatedly accept new bodies, giving up old ones.

From time immemorial, the eternal soul has thus been wandering within the material world, taking on temporary material bodies one after another, each time forgetting the previous one, and thinking the present one to be all-in-all.

The *Padma Purāṇa* says that there are 84 lakh species of life in the material world:

jala-jā nava-lakṣāṇi
sthāvarā lakṣa-viṁśati
kṛmayo rudra-saṅkhyakāḥ
pakṣiṇāṁ daśa-lakṣaṇam
triṁśal-lakṣāṇi paśavaḥ
catur-lakṣāṇi mānuṣāḥ

(*Padma Purāṇa*)

Aquatics	9 lakh species
Trees and Plants	20 lakh species
Insects and Reptiles	11 lakh species
Birds	10 lakh species
Animals	30 lakh species
Human Beings	4 lakh species
TOTAL	84 LAKH SPECIES

These species embody different levels of consciousness.

- Even amongst human beings, there are 4 lakh species (based on levels of consciousness).

- The meaning of word 'species' in biology is used in a different sense from the one used in the *Vedas*.

- In modern science, species is categorized according to its superficial morphological appearance and thus, a cat and a tiger may be treated as belonging to the same family because they look similar.

- **But the *Vedas* categorize species according to their guṇas or qualities. There are three qualities: *sattva-guṇa* (mode of goodness), *rajo-guṇa* (mode of passion) and *tamo-guṇa* (mode of ignorance). These three are mixed together in various permutations and combinations to arrive at 84 lakh species with varied consciousness.**

- Sometimes the soul may occupy a human body, sometimes an insect's body, sometimes a bird's body or sometimes even a demigod's body.

- In this way, the soul keeps revolving round-and-round in the wheel of Saṁsāra, the cycle of birth and death, amongst the 84 lakh species of life.

This evolution is quite different from the Evolution Theory of Charles Darwin (that man has evolved from the Apes), which is a highly speculative and erroneous idea, not in conformity with scriptures.

Darwin speculated about some type of 'evolution', which involves one type of species evolving into a higher type of species. Since the word 'species' in modern science refers to the external morphological appearance and characteristics, as mentioned earlier, what Darwin suggested was that it was the body itself that changed or 'evolved' over a period of time into a body of a higher level.

- **The fact, however, is that we have never seen any simple organism developing into a higher form of life.**

- **We have never seen any species of life giving birth to another higher than itself.**
- **For example, we do not see amphibians reproducing reptiles or monkeys reproducing humans.**
- **Moreover, if one physical species actually did evolve into a higher species, that lower species should have disappeared. How is it that all species of life co-exist today?**

And, as far as the "evidence" for the Darwinian Theory of Evolution like the fossils is considered, well, that is another story, which cannot be explained in detail here. It's sufficient to say here that vast amounts of evidence that would contradict the Evolution Theory have been screened out and the record of the fossils has been carefully edited to support it. For example, many fossils show the presence of 'modern' man throughout a vast span of time, even at periods when, the Evolution Theory says, not "modern man" but his ape-like "ancestors" should have lived.

Therefore, Darwin's Theory of Evolution is unacceptable. Instead, we accept 'evolution' in the sense of the soul's movement into different bodies, one after another.

The souls move higher automatically in the hierarchy of the 84 lakh species one by one, and then come to the human form of life.

The human species is a junction for the soul.

According to *karma* performed in the human body, the next birth may be either in the lower species, in the higher species (i.e., the demigods), or in the human species.

And if the human being has attained spiritual perfection, then the soul can be released from the cycle of birth and death and return to the spiritual world, the kingdom of God - Vaikuṇṭha.

4.3. LIFE EXISTS ALL OVER THE UNIVERSE

Every environment in the universe, in different planets, is capable of sustaining life forms and there are living beings in appropriate bodies in all planets.

The soul has been described as "*sarva-gataḥ*" in *Bhagavad-gītā*.

acchedyo 'yam adāhyo 'yam
akledyo 'śoṣya eva ca
nityaḥ sarva-gataḥ sthāṇur
acalo 'yaṁ sanātanaḥ
(*Bhagavad-gītā* 2.24)

Translation: *"This individual soul is unbreakable and insoluble, and can be neither burned nor dried. He is everlasting, present everywhere, unchangeable, immovable and eternally the same."*

Srila Prabhupada in his commentary on this verse explains:

"The word *sarva-gataḥ* ("all pervading") is significant because there is no doubt that living entities are all over God's creation. They live on the land, in the water, in the air, within the earth and even within fire.

The belief that they are sterilized in fire is not acceptable, because it is clearly stated here that the soul cannot be burned by fire. Therefore, there is no doubt that there are living entities also in the sun planet with suitable bodies to live there. If the sun globe is uninhabited, then the word *sarva-gataḥ* - "living everywhere" - becomes meaningless."

Modern research has confirmed that there are some types of germs living in boiling water and even in fire! So it is not difficult to accept that life could exist on different planets of the universe in appropriate life form.

Even on our tiny planet earth we see that the fish have one kind of body to be able to live in the water, the birds have a body appropriate for the air, and humans for the land.

Similarly, in other planets there are bodies made differently according to the atmosphere there and all these are obtained according to one's *karma*.

4.4. THE GARMENT SHOP OF MATERIAL NATURE

We have already seen that the material body is like a dress for the soul. Since there are 84 lakh species in the world, it means that there are as many varieties of 'dresses' available for the soul to 'wear' in the 'garment shop' of Material Nature.

The living entity 'chooses' a particular 'dress' according to its desire, as expressed through its activities (*karma*) and material nature then awards that body to the soul.

The *karma* performed is the 'price' with which the soul can 'purchase' the new body. For every kind of desire, there is an appropriate 'dress' or body available in the large 'shop' of material nature. Such is the elaborate arrangement of God.

4.5. EAT MEAT? BECOME A TIGER...

- The pure spirit soul belongs to the spiritual world, Vaikuṇṭha. He is not meant to be here in this material world. But somehow or other, he has come here and, since time immemorial, has been struggling against the stringent laws of material nature, accepting body after body.
- The living entity is supposed to lead a pure life with such desires and activities that will liberate him from this vicious Wheel of Saṁsāra.
- However, out of ignorance, he does not understand what kinds of desires and activities will actually bring about his welfare. So he acts in most unbecoming ways, against his real interest, and suffers.
- Being captivated and allured by the attractions of the false pleasures of this world, he becomes a bundle of illicit desires. Material nature then forcibly awards him that material body which exactly corresponds to his desires and activities.
- Each kind of body in nature is designed to efficiently cater to certain kinds of desires. For example, a bear's body is perfectly suited for excessive sleep. The tiger's body is just right for eating meat. Monkeys have a prolific capacity for engaging in sex, in a measure that is not possible for humans. The human body, however, is meant for God–realization alone. That is its uniqueness and specialty, not found in any other kind of body.
- Having obtained the human form of life, if one neglects the sublime path of God-realization and instead lives a degraded life dedicated merely to animalistic pursuits, one may forfeit the right to get a human body in the next birth.
- **"Want to eat meat? Take a tiger's body!", says material nature.**
- **"Love sleeping excessively? Here's a bear's body for you!".**
- **"Like exposing your body? Become a tree!"**

- **In this way, material nature gives us bodies just appropriate to our desires and activities.**

We have seen earlier that there are two kinds of material bodies:

- The gross body made up of earth, water, fire, air and ether, and
- The subtle body made up of mind, intelligence and false ego.

The gross body is the 'outer dress' for the soul and the subtle body is the 'inner dress'. At the time of death, the soul gives up the gross body i.e. outer dress, but the subtle body or inner dress remains.

- It is, in fact, the subtle body that acts as a vehicle to carry the soul from the old body to the new body. The subtle body, which harbors the desires of the living entity, carries the conception of the next body, and it develops another gross body in the next life. Lord Kṛṣṇa compares this transfer to the way air carries aromas from one place to another.

- Under the superintendence of the Supersoul, the minute spirit soul then enters into the womb of a particular mother through the semen of a father and develops a particular type of body supplied by the mother.

4.6. THE LAW OF KARMA

According to the Law of *Karma*, for every action that an individual performs, there is an appropriate reaction. This is a subtle law that governs all the activities of living beings.

There is a similar law in modern science, ("every action has an equal and opposite reaction").

The Law of *Karma* is a law of cause and effect or action and reaction. This means that for everything we do there will be a reaction, and for everything that is happening there is a past cause (known or unknown).

Thus one can understand that we are presently suffering or enjoying the fruits of our past activities and that our present activities will determine our future suffering or enjoyment.

No one can escape this law, however big or small he may be. And certainly, ignorance of the law is no excuse.

It works perfectly under the control of God, acting through material nature and time.

4.7. THREE KINDS OF ACTIVITIES

In the *Bhagavad-gītā*, Lord Kṛṣṇa explains that there are three kinds of activities one can perform:

karmaṇo hy api boddhavyaṁ
boddhavyaṁ ca vikarmaṇaḥ
akarmaṇaś ca boddhavyaṁ
gahanā karmaṇo gatiḥ
(*Bhagavad-gītā* 4.17)

Translation: "*The intricacies of action are very hard to understand. Therefore, one should know properly what action is, what forbidden action is, and what inaction is.*"

This is represented in the chart below:

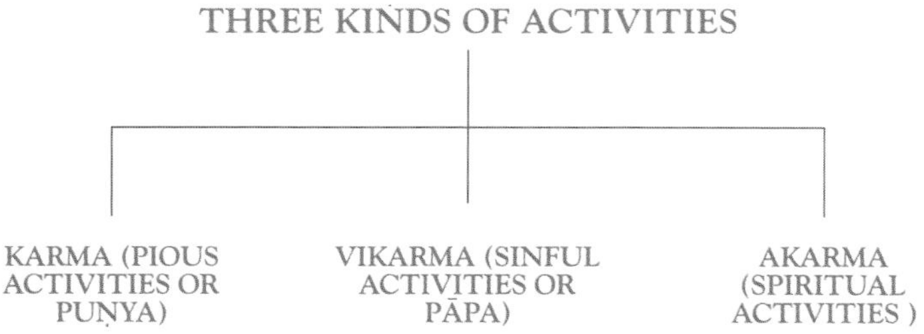

4.8. PIOUS ACTIVITY (KARMA)

- The word "*Karma*" generally means 'any action'.
- However, there is also another specific meaning, namely, pious activity, also called puṇya.
- **Puṇya refers to those activities, which are prescribed and sanctioned by the Lord through the scriptures. Performance of such activities gives one material benefits in return.**

- In other words, these are pious credits, the results of which the performer will enjoy in this life or the next.
- Example of pious activities are: giving charity to the poor, helping the blind, distributing free medicines, digging wells, planting trees, feeding the hungry and so on.
- **By performing such pious activities one may attain in the future lives wealth, beauty, good birth, health, material happiness and even birth in the heavenly planets.**

4.9. SINFUL ACTIVITY (VIKARMA)

- ***Vikarma*** **or sin refers to prohibited actions, i.e. those actions which violate the scriptural injunctions, which go against the principles and rules given by God for civilized human society.** Sin is usually performed out of ignorance, and leads to suffering in this life and the next.
- Examples of sin are stealing, killing, indulging in vices like drinking alcohol, eating meat and so on.
- **By performing sin, one attains suffering, poverty, disease, low birth, ugliness etc.**

4.10. BOTH KARMA AND VIKARMA ARE THE CAUSE OF BONDAGE

It is important to note that both *karma* and *vikarma* are material activities and they bind one to the cycle of birth and death because they force us to take birth again to enjoy or suffer their reactions.

When one continuously performs puṇya one accumulates one's stock of puṇya, which stands to one's credit. As a result of this, one gets an opportunity in the future, to enjoy material facilities and happiness (say, in the heavenly planets).

And as one enjoys, the stock of puṇya gets depleted. When the stock is exhausted, one has to return to one's original position (on earth). As Lord Kṛṣṇa explains:

te taṁ bhuktvā svarga-lokaṁ viśālaṁ
kṣīṇe puṇye martya-lokaṁ viśanti
evaṁ trayī-dharmam anuprapannā
gatāgataṁ kāma-kāmā labhante
(*Bhagavad-gītā* 9.21)

Translation: "*When they have thus enjoyed vast heavenly sense pleasure and the results of their pious activities are exhausted, they return to this mortal planet again. Thus those who seek sense enjoyment by adhering to the principles of the three Vedas achieve only repeated birth and death.*"

Here is an example to help us understand this point:

- A businessman may work very hard for some time and accumulate a lot of money. Then he decides to take a vacation and enjoy himself. As he enjoys, he has to spend his hard earned money. Eventually, when his stock of money has depleted, he has to return to working hard in his business once again. Similarly, by performing pious activity, one gets the fruit in terms of material happiness, etc. and then one returns to one's earlier state.
- Similar logic holds good for sinful activity. Consider a criminal who is jailed for one year for committing a crime. As he suffers in the jail, with every passing day his 'stock' of crime reduces, and finally at the end of one year, he is free once again to return to his earlier position.

Exactly like that, when one performs sinful activity, one may be punished by being sent to the hellish planets for certain duration of time. By enduring this punishment, one depletes one's stock of sin and eventually returns to one's earlier position.

In this way, by enjoying, one exhausts the results of one's puṇya, and by suffering, one exhausts the results of one's sins.

Since one goes on performing pious and sinful activities, one is forced to repeatedly take birth in order to enjoy and suffer the fruits of one's activities. Thus the Wheel of Saṁsāra rotates.

4.11. AKARMA

'*Akarma*', literally means 'inaction,' But this does not mean a physical cessation of actions or avoidance of work.

Akarma **refers to spiritual activities, i.e. activities performed on behalf of or for the pleasure of God.**

Because they are so performed, without selfish desire, they do not implicate the performer or entangle him.

In other words, *akarma* does not bring material reactions.

Examples of this are: Chanting the names of God, worshipping Him and serving Him and other acts of *Bhakti*.

By *akarma*, one develops devotion for the Lord, detachment from worldly affairs, purity and spiritual happiness.

Akarma liberates one from the cycle of birth and death and takes one back to the spiritual world. Kṛṣṇa explains in the *Bhagavad-gītā*:

yajñārthāt karmaṇo 'nyatra
loko 'yaṁ karma-bandhanaḥ
tad-arthaṁ karma kaunteya
mukta-saṅgaḥ samācara

(*Bhagavad-gītā* 3.9)

हरे कृष्ण

Translation: *"Work done as a sacrifice for Viṣṇu has to be performed; otherwise work causes bondage in this material world. Therefore, O son of Kuntī, perform your prescribed duties for His satisfaction, and in that way you will always remain free from bondage."*

4.12. PUṆYA (KARMA) & SPIRITUAL ACTIVITY (AKARMA) ARE NOT THE SAME

People commonly imagine "puṇya" or ordinary pious activity to be spiritual activity (*akarma*).

But the two are actually quite different and it is important to be clear in our mind about this difference.

- **Puṇya (*karma*) is 'good' material activity, pertaining to the material body.**

- By performing this, one can get promoted to a better material situation within the material world, but one cannot go beyond it, just like in the case of a prisoner who may be transferred to a better jail cell with more facilities, but who is not allowed to leave the jail.
- *Akarma* or devotional service to the Lord, on the other hand, being fully spiritual, has nothing to do with this material world.
- It is on the platform of the soul.
- *Bhakti* is not meant for material promotion but it is meant to transfer us to the spiritual world beyond the cycle of birth and death.

Akarma **is thus beyond both *karma* and *vikarma*.**

4.13. INSTANT AND DELAYED KARMA

I) We have seen that for every action we perform, there is a reaction. The reaction may come immediately or after some time, or even after a very long time.

For example :

- **A thief caught stealing on the street will face an immediate reaction.** This is instant *karma*.
- **Eating contaminated food will bring its reaction (an upset stomach) a few hours later.** This is slightly delayed *karma*.
- **A clever murderer may go undetected and be caught only after several months and then punished.** Karmic reaction here is further delayed.
- **The reaction to an illicit activity may come even twenty years later (e.g. AIDS).** This is *karma* that is still further delayed.

II) In this way, we can extend this logic to understand that karmic reactions for actions performed now, may come even in future life times.

This is a crucial point to understand.

Many people however, want to know why reactions to our *karma* do not all come in this life itself. Why the spill-over to future lives, they ask. So let's see, why.

4.14. THE LOGIC FOR BELIEVING THAT REACTIONS TO OUR KARMA MAY COME IN FUTURE LIVES

Some karmic reactions do certainly come in the same life, but there are many that do not. So here's why we say that karmic reactions may even come in future lives.

I) Death interrupts the fructifying of our *karma*

- We perform so many activities every day. Each *karma* must bring its own reaction as per the Law of *Karma*. And all the reactions do not come immediately as we have seen. So, at any given moment, there will be so many karmic reactions we are yet to receive. **Therefore, at the moment of death, there will always be a stock of unfructified karmic reactions.**
- Since death has interrupted the natural action – reaction flow, it is evident that we will have to take a next birth to receive those karmic reactions.

II) Different karmic seeds take different time to fructify

- Every *karma* we perform is like a seed that we sow. Every seed has its own nature that makes it bear fruit at a certain time.
- **If we plant seeds of papaya, mango, neem and apple etc., each will produce fruit at different times according to its intrinsic nature. One may bear fruit very soon and another very late, after several years.**
- Similarly all karmic seeds will not bear fruit at the same time; rather, following their intrinsic quality (i.e. depending on the nature of the ***karma***), they will fructify at different times.

■ Some karmic seeds naturally take a short time to fructify, and some a long time. Therefore, according to their nature some karmic reactions may come in this life and some in future lives.

III) Conditions have to be right

■ Some karmic reactions can come only in certain situations. And if those situations do not presently prevail, the reactions will have to wait for the right time.

■ A story will illustrate this point. A certain hunter killed 100 birds even as the parents were alive. The hunter was to suffer for this sin by seeing his own 100 sons dying before him. But scripture says that one can obtain a son only when one has a certain stock of 'puṇya'. The hunter had to perform many, many pious activities in future lives in order to accumulate the piety required for having 100 sons. This took no less than 50 lifetimes. In this new life, the (former) hunter was now eligible to receive the karmic reactions of killing the 100 birds. He had to suffer the agony of his 100 sons dying before him. This man was none other than King Dhṛtarāṣṭra, father of the Kauravas.

■ Hence, Lord Kṛṣṇa declares in the *Bhagavad-gītā* (4.17): *gahanā karmaṇo gatiḥ*, i.e. the intricacies of *karma* are very hard to understand.

IV) Body is only a dress

■ A thief may commit a crime when he is wearing a white shirt and is arrested a few days later when he is wearing, say, a red shirt. Does the color of his shirt make any difference? After all, the person is the same and he must suffer punishment regardless of what clothes he is wearing.

■ Similarly, since the body is only a dress for the soul, it does not matter whether the reactions comes when the same dress is being worn (i.e. in the same life) or a different dress (i.e. some future life). Isn't it very simple and sublime logic?

V) Forgetfulness of the cause is no excuse

- **A thief may take the plea that he does not remember having committed a particular theft, but if found guilty he will still be punished.**
- Similarly, our forgetfulness of the cause, of our suffering or enjoyment, will not alter it. Even though we may not remember, there are higher authorities in this universe who keep record and do remember. Hence, the karmic reactions will certainly come in an appropriate life, when the time is right.

4.15. CAN GOOD KARMA CANCEL BAD KARMA

Generally, one must face the reactions for good *karma* (puṇya) and bad *karma* (sin) separately, i.e. 'good' reactions for the good *karma* and 'bad' reactions for the 'bad' *karma*.

The story of King Nṛga mistakenly giving in charity the same cow to two different *brāhmaṇas*; is appropriate in this regard. As a result of the sin, the king had to take the body of a lizard and as a result of his pious activities he ascended later to the heavenly planets. This story appears in the *Śrīmad-Bhāgavatam.*

There is however, a system of '*prāyaścitta*' or 'atonement' available in the *Karma Kanda* section of the *Vedas* by which certain kinds of sinful reactions may be nullified or mitigated by performance of certain ritualistic pious activities for atonement.

Although the sinful reactions may be counteracted successfully in this manner, the propensity to commit sin does not disappear.

Hence, one performs sinful activity again and again, and remains bound to the material world.

Unlimitedly more beneficial than this ritualistic atonement process is the path of *Bhakti* to Lord Kṛṣṇa as the great sage Śukadeva

Gosvāmī declares in the *Śrīmad-Bhāgavatam*:

kecit kevalayā bhaktyā
vāsudeva-parāyaṇāḥ
aghaṁ dhunvanti kārtsnyena
nīhāram iva bhāskaraḥ
(*Śrīmad-Bhāgavatam* 6.1.15)

Translation: "*Only a rare person who has adopted complete, unalloyed devotional service to Kṛṣṇa can uproot the weeds of sinful actions with no possibility that they will revive. He can do this simply by discharging devotional service, just as the sun can immediately dissipate fog by its rays.*"

4.16. INDIVIDUAL AND COLLECTIVE KARMA

While we all have to individually face the reactions of our *karma*, the sum total of the *karma* a of certain group of people may also affect the group as a whole.

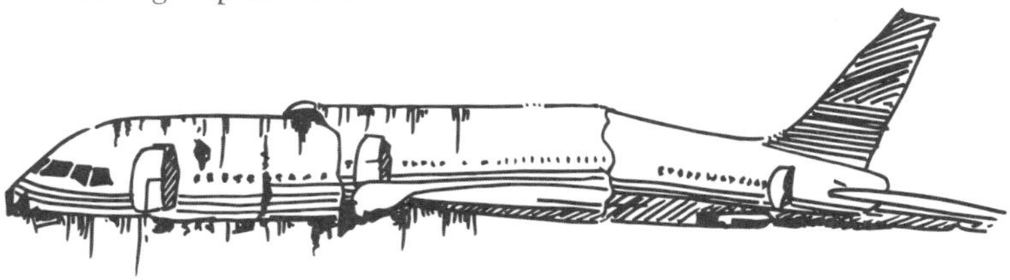

Examples are: plane crashes, earth quakes etc, where people in large numbers suffer similar kind of fate.

Their *karma* has brought them all together to die in a certain manner.

4.17. PRĀRABDHA KARMA AND SANCHITA KARMA

'*Sanchita karma*' is the sum total of all our past karmic reactions.

***Prarabdha karma* is that portion of our karmic reactions that has fallen due to us in this lifetime.**

It is according to *prārabdha karma* that one is born in a certain family, with a certain kind of body, with certain amount of happiness and distress, a certain kind of death and so on.

4.18. WHAT IS DESTINY OR FATE?

Destiny is nothing but the aggregate of karmic reactions that have presently borne fruit or will shortly bear fruit.

The destiny for our present life is simply our *prārabdha* karma.

Therefore, it is truly said, "Man is the maker of his own destiny."

4.19. IS THERE SCOPE FOR FREE WILL?

People ask: "If everything is destined, do we have any free will at all"?

Firstly, not everything is destined. **Destiny is what happens to us as a result of our past activities. That cannot be avoided.**

But our free will lies in how we respond to that and generally how we act in life. Free will is never destroyed.

However, our destiny (habits and attitudes) born out of association (of many years, and indeed, many lifetimes) may influence the way we use our free will.

So we should try to cultivate good spiritual company so that we can develop good habits healthy, positive attitude and proper spiritual desires.

Then the exercise of our free will leads us to perfection in life.

4.20. CHOICE EXISTS BEFORE PERFORMING KARMA, NOT AFTER

Every *karma* we perform is like:

- **a word spoken**
- **an arrow shot or**
- **a bullet fired**

Once done, it is done. It cannot be changed. It must, in due course of time, bring its reaction.

Our choice or free-will exists before we perform the *karma*. Once we perform it, we have no choice but to accept the reaction.

Consider, for instance, that a man has jumped off of a building. Before he jumped, he had a choice to jump or not to jump.

But once he has jumped, he no longer has any choice; he must face the reaction of the jump. Death is his destiny, but it became so only after he exercised his choice, and jumped.

This is what destiny is all about, Destiny is simply the sum total of karmic reactions waiting for us. That we may not remember, what action caused a particular reaction, is not relevant.

In other words, destiny is the product of the use (or misuse) of our own free-will. We have no one to blame but ourselves for our sufferings. Who can we blame when we bite our own tongue?

Now, we are in a position to answer the following question that people commonly ask.

4.21. WHY DO BAD THINGS HAPPEN TO GOOD PEOPLE

The answer is: because these 'good' people had done something 'bad' in previous lives and are now facing these reactions as their destiny. For the 'good' actions that they are doing now, they will receive the 'good' reactions in the future. After all, every action will lead to an appropriate reaction.

Of course, people generally perform a mixture of 'good' and 'bad' *karma*, so the reactions also come in mixed form.

Using the same reasoning, we can understand why good things happen to bad people.

We can understand this easily with the example of a 'Silo', which is a container to store grain.

Fresh grain is added periodically from the top and the grain for daily use is removed regularly from on opening at the bottom.

Consider that in a particular year, there was bad grain and in the next year the grain harvested was of good quality.

In the second year when the farmer uses grain for his personal consumption, he may continue to get inferior quality grain even though he has put superior quality grain in the Silo. This is because the stock of the inferior grain of the previous year has not been exhausted.

Similarly, even if we are living 'good' lives now, we may experience many miseries if our stock of past 'bad' *karma* has not been exhausted. Once that is done, however, then the stock of our present 'good *karma*' will begin to bear fruit.

4.22. FREEDOM FROM KARMA / VIKARMA

As we have seen earlier, both 'good' *karma* (puṇya) and 'bad' *karma* (sin) are causes of bondage to this material world.

It is only by surrendering to Lord Kṛṣṇa, and engaging in His devotional service we can become completely free from this miserable bondage of the Law of *Karma*.

Thus, after death we can return home, to the kingdom of God for an eternal life of bliss.

5. MATERIAL NATURE & TIME

CHAPTER 5

MATERIAL NATURE & TIME

5.1. WHAT IS PRAKṚTI (MATERIAL NATURE)

The Supreme Lord is "*Puruṣa*" (i.e. Enjoyer) and everything else is '*prakṛti*' (i.e. that which is to be enjoyed).

Prakṛti is of two kinds:

Material energy which is called *aparā prakṛti* (or inferior energy of God) and, Spiritual energy which is called *parā prakṛti* (or superior energy of God).

The material energy consists of eight elements: earth, water, fire, air, ether, mind, intelligence and false ego.

The spiritual energy within this world is the aggregate of all the individual spirit souls.

'*Prakṛti*' means "energy". Both the *prakṛtis* (energies), material and spiritual, are meant to be engaged in the service of the Supreme Energetic Kṛṣṇa, Who is the source of all energies.

The material world is constituted of the material energy but is being sustained by the spiritual energy (i.e. the souls) who are wandering in different species of life.

Generally, however, the word '*prakṛti*' refers to the material energy and we will use this word in this sense here.

This is one of the five subjects discussed in the *Bhagavad-gītā*.

5.2. OUR UNIVERSE

Let us learn in brief what our Vedic scriptures say about our universe:

- **Our universe is very large in size and is egg-shaped. Thus it is called 'Brahmāṇḍa'.**

- **The covering of the universe has seven layers, each made of different elements, and each outer layer being ten times thicker than the one immediately preceding it.**

- Inside the space of this 'egg', there are 14 levels of planetary systems. Our planetary system is called Bhūloka and it is in the middle.

- Above this are the six higher planetary systems: Bhuvarloka, Svargloka, Maharloka, Janaloka, Tapoloka and finally, Satyaloka which is the topmost. In each of these planetary systems, there are many planets, each having appropriate life forms.

- **Below the Bhūloka there are the seven lower planetary systems: Atala, Vitala, Sutala, Talātala, Mahātala, Rasātala and Pātāla.**

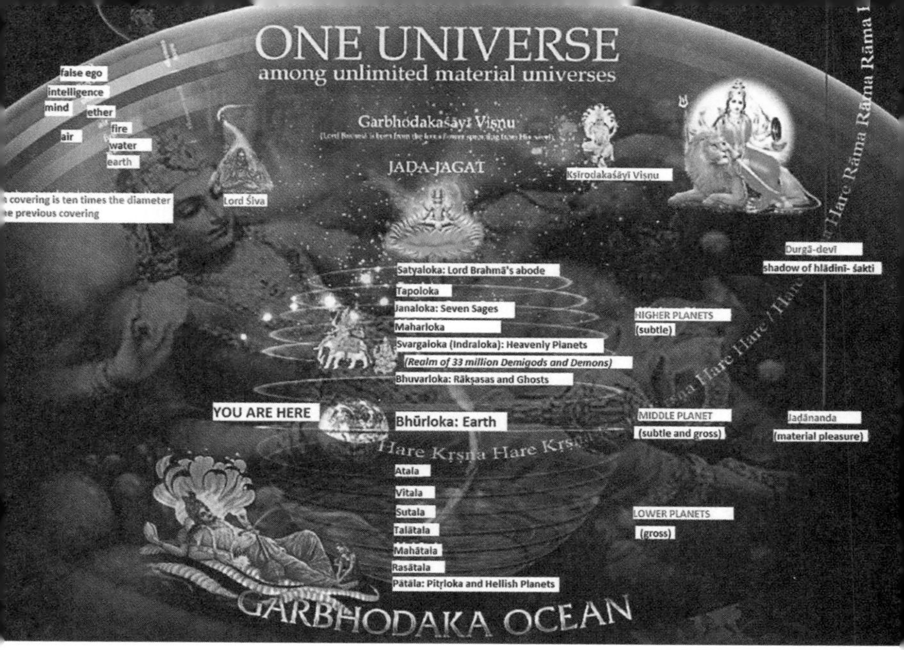

■ **In all these 14 planetary systems there is birth and death. As Lord Kṛṣṇa says:**

ā-brahma-bhuvanāl lokāḥ
punar āvartino 'rjuna
mām upetya tu kaunteya
punar janma na vidyate
(*Bhagavad-gītā* 8.16)

Translation: *"From the highest planet in the material world down to the lowest, all are places of misery wherein repeated birth and deaths take place. But one who attains to My abode, O son of Kuntī, never takes birth again."*

■ **In addition to these, there are many varieties of hellish planets located even below the 14 planetary systems.** This is where very sinful human beings are sent for appropriate punishment. That is a preparation for their next births in lower species of life on earth.

5.3. THE WHOLE MATERIAL CREATION

Our universe is only one tiny universe amongst million of others, many of which are far bigger than ours.

Our universe is thus like a tiny mustard seed in a large bag of mustard seeds. All these universes together constitute the entire material world.

In every universe, there is a Brahmā, who is empowered for the task of creation and Lord Śiva who is empowered for the task of destruction. Lord Kṛṣṇa personally takes charge of sustaining the universe in His form as Viṣṇu, because sustaining is the most difficult part.

This means that, there are as many Brahmās, Viṣṇus and Śivas as there are material universes.

Śrī Caitanya Mahāprabhu narrated one incident about the four-headed Brahmā of our universe approaching Lord Kṛṣṇa in Dvārakā. When Brahmā entered Lord Kṛṣṇa's room, he was astonished to see millions of other Brahmās and Śivas with large number of heads and countless Indras also. Other Brahmās and Śivas, by Kṛṣṇa's mystic potency could not see any other Brahmā, or Śiva. Only our four-headed Brahmā, by Kṛṣṇa's special arrangement could see the others. All the Brahmās, Śivas and others offered their respects to Kṛṣṇa and with the latter's blessings, they departed.

Lord Kṛṣṇa explained to the four-headed Brahmā, that his universe was the smallest among the vast multitude of universes, each of which was very large. The larger the universe, the larger the number of heads of Brahmā in that universe. Thus there were Brahmās with thousands and even millions of heads, whose universes were trillions and trillions of miles wide.

We can thus understand, how absolutely tiny and insignificant we are in this material creation. This should bring about a sense of humility in all of us and make us realize how petty our worldly ambitions and plans are.

5.4. EACH UNIVERSE IS CREATED, MAINTAINED AND DESTROYED

All the universes are created, sustained for a while and then destroyed. This cycle of creation, maintenance and destruction goes on eternally.

- **All these universes are a manifestation of *prakṛti*, the material energy.**
- **When the universes are destroyed, *prakṛti* returns to its original, unmanifest state.**
- **It is then again activated and the universes are once more created, only to be destroyed after a while. In this way, the cycle goes on.**
- **It is important to note here that *prakṛti*, being inert, or not conscious, cannot act on its own. It needs the superior direction and control of the Lord.**
- **Furthermore, while the universes themselves are temporary because they are created, sustained and destroyed, the *prakṛti*, on the other hand, is eternal.**

Let's see a simple example to understand these points.

5.5. PRAKṚTI IS ETERNAL BUT THE MATERIAL WORLD IS NOT

Consider the following: mud, a mud pot and a potter. The potter makes many pots out of mud. These pots remain for some time and eventually break. The mud that constitutes the pot mixes back with the original mud. Once again the potter makes pots with the mud and the cycle repeats.

We see here that the pots come and go, but the mud remains. The various forms into which the mud is transformed change, but the mud remains, whether before the pots are made, while the pots exist, or after the pots are destroyed.

Furthermore, we also note that the mud cannot transform into pots on its own. The expert hands of a potter are required.

- ***Prakṛti*** **(or material energy) is like the mud.**
- **The innumerable material universes are like the mud pots.**
- **God is like the potter.**

Therefore, the conclusion is that:

A) God exists eternally.

B) *Prakṛti* exists eternally.

C) The material world, consisting of transformation of the *prakṛti*, is temporary.

Prakṛti is inert and not conscious. It needs the Supreme Conscious Being, God, or Lord Kṛṣṇa to activate it just as the mud needs the potter and the material body needs the soul.

What lies beyond this *prakṛti* and the vast multitude of material universes? It is the Spiritual World, Vaikuṇṭha. Let us learn something about it.

5.6. THE SPIRITUAL WORLD

In the 8th chapter of the *Bhagavad-gītā*, after Lord Kṛṣṇa has explained the cyclical nature of this material creation, He speaks about the world beyond, the spiritual world:

paras tasmāt tu bhāvo 'nyo
'vyakto 'vyaktāt sanātanaḥ
yaḥ sa sarveṣu bhūteṣu
naśyatsu na vinaśyati
(***Bhagavad-gītā*** 8.20)

Translation: *"Yet there is another unmanifest nature, which is eternal and is transcendental to this manifested and unmanifested matter. It is supreme and is never annihilated. When all in this world is annihilated, that part remains as it is."*

avyakto 'kṣara ity uktas
tam āhuḥ paramāṁ gatim
yaṁ prāpya na nivartante
tad dhāma paramaṁ mama
(***Bhagavad-gītā*** 8.21)

Translation: *"That which the Vedāntists describe as unmanifest and infallible, that which is known as the supreme destination, that place from which, having attained it, one never returns- that is My supreme abode."*

The important points being made by Lord Kṛṣṇa in these verses are:

A) Beyond this temporary material creation is another abode that is eternal, that is not destroyed when the material world is destroyed.

B) That eternal realm is Lord Kṛṣṇa's own, personal, supreme abode ('*tad dhāma paramaṁ mama*'); and

C) One who attains to that abode, never returns here, to this material world.

Lord Kṛṣṇa gives us a further glimpse into His Kingdom in *Bhagavad-gītā:*

na tad bhāsayate sūryo
na śaśāṅko na pāvakaḥ
yad gatvā na nivartante
tad dhāma paramaṁ mama
(**Bhagavad-gītā** 15.6)

Translation: *"That supreme abode of Mine is not illumined by the sun or moon, nor by fire or electricity. Those who reach it never return to this material world."*

- The abode of the Lord is self-effulgent.
- The Kingdom of God is made up entirely of spiritual energy.
- There is no trace of the material energy there.
- It is eternal, full of knowledge and full of bliss.
- In that spiritual world, Vaikuṇṭha, there are unlimited spiritual planets, each unimaginably vast in size. They are called Vaikuṇṭha- lokas.
- The largest and most important among them all is called Goloka Vṛndāvana or Kṛṣṇaloka where Lord Kṛṣṇa in His original, two-handed, flute-playing form, resides.

Kṛṣṇa expands Himself into innumerable four-handed Nārāyaṇa forms, each of whom presides over a particular Vaikuṇṭha-loka. Unlimited devotees in pure spiritual form reside in these spiritual planets serving the Supreme Lord with great devotion and enjoying unparalleled bliss in His association.

When it comes to dealing with the material creation, The original Supreme Personality of Godhead, Sri Kṛṣṇa, does not get personally or directly involved.

Through a series of expansions, He manifests Himself in various Viṣṇu forms, Who then do the needful. **These Viṣṇu forms who are non- different from Kṛṣṇa, are thus like "office" forms of Kṛṣṇa, who do the "official" work of seeing the creation, sustenance and destruction of the material creation.**

There are three main Viṣṇu forms in this regard:

- Mahā-Viṣṇu
- Garbhodakaśāyī Viṣṇu, and
- Kṣīrodakaśāyī Viṣṇu

Let us see what role each of these plays in the material creation.

5.7. MAHĀ-VIṢṆU - THE SOURCE OF THE MATERIAL WORLD

Lord Kṛṣṇa in the spiritual world, after a series of expansions assumes the extraordinary gigantic form of Mahā-Viṣṇu.

- **Mahā-Viṣṇu lies in the Causal Ocean in one corner of the spiritual sky.**
- **As He breathes out, innumerable universes emanates from Him through the pores of His skin. So we can only imagine how large Mahā-Viṣṇu is.**

These universes grow and move outwards and appear like tiny bubbles in the Causal Ocean.

The process of creation takes place in every universe (as will be described later) and each universe is also maintained for the duration of Mahā-Viṣṇu's exhalation (i.e., outward breathing).

The life span of each universe is very large but it is equivalent to only one breath of Mahā-Viṣṇu.

When Mahā-Viṣṇu inhales, all the universes enter back into Him and are destroyed. The material energy and all the souls in the material world remain dormant in Him till the time of next creation.

When Mahā-Viṣṇu breathes out again, the creation takes place once again. In this way, the material world undergoes an eternal cycle of creation, sustenance and destruction.

5.8. CREATION WITHIN EACH UNIVERSE

As the universes emerge from Mahā-Viṣṇu's gigantic, divine form during His exhaling, the same Mahā-Viṣṇu expands Himself into as many forms as there are universes, and enters into each universe. This form of Lord is called Garbhodakaśāyī Viṣṇu. This is the second level of the Viṣṇu form in the material creation.

Garbhodakaśāyī Viṣṇu fills half the universe with His own perspiration (the Lord's perspiration is not like ours!) and lies down in it using the great serpent *avatāra*, Ananta Śeṣa, as His bed. His divine consort Lakṣmī devī serves Him constantly and devotedly.

From His navel comes a lotus flower, having a long stem. On top of that extraordinary lotus is born another extraordinary being - Brahmā.

Brahmā, as we have seen earlier, is generally a *jīvātmā*, (an ordinary spirit soul) who has been elevated to that post due to heaps of pious activities performed in the past.

The Brahmā of our universe has four heads. In other universes which are much larger, there are Brahmās with many more heads - ten, hundred, thousand......and so on.

Please recall the story of Brahmā, visiting Dvārakā, narrated earlier.

We should remember that this event takes place in every universe.

5.9. BRAHMĀ AS CREATOR

When Brahmā is born on the lotus flower, he is bewildered and confused. He does not know what to do. He wonders where he is, and what is around him. He also seeks to know how should he create the universe. He moves up and down the stem of that extraordinary lotus but still does not find the answer.

Then he hears a voice which he cannot identify, that advises him to perform penance.

In accordance with that instruction, Brahmā, performs penances for a very long time.

Being pleased with Brahmā, the Lord appears before him and guides him, both from within and without.

Upon being blessed in this way by the personal audience and instructions of the Lord, Brahmā, now is ready to begin the task of creation.

Being empowered by the Lord with special potency, he creates all the living beings and distributes them on different planets after creating them. The fourteen levels of planetary systems are all located in the stem of that wonderful lotus.

Thus Brahmā acts like a gardener, sowing the seeds (of the living entities) given by the Lord in appropriate soils (i.e. bodies and planets), all according to their *karma* from the previous creation.

Even though Brahmā's intelligence and ability is extremely great, yet he cannot fully comprehend exactly how the Lord's energies work so wonderfully to bring about this creation. In front of the Supreme Lord, Brahmā feels himself insignificant.

The progeny of Brahmā create further progeny and in this way the universe is populated with the 84 lakh species of life.

FEAR OF DEATH
ANGER AFTER FRUSTRATION
SENSE OF FALSE OWNERSHIP
BODILY CONCEPTION
GREED
PULASTYA
PURANAS
MEDICAL SCIENCE
POWER OF SPEAKING
KRATU
ATHARVA
ṚK
SĀMA
VASIṢṬHA
AṄGIRĀ
ya-ra-la-va
sa-ṣa-sa-ha
DAKṢA
NĀRADA
PULAHA
KARDAMA

5.10. THE THIRD EXPANSION OF VIṢṆU

Garbhodakaśāyī Viṣṇu expands Himself to become Kṣīrodakaśāyī Viṣṇu, who resides on a planet called śveta-dvīpa within the universe, in the ocean of milk (Kṣīra-sāgara). He lies down on Ananta Śeṣa and has Lakṣmī devī serving Him.

Kṣīrodakaśāyī Viṣṇu is the Viṣṇu commonly known as part of the trinity Brahmā, Viṣṇu and Śiva.

He sustains the whole universe by His inconceivable potency.

When the demigods are in trouble, they approach Him on the banks of the milk ocean and offer prayers.

The Lord then responds to alleviate their troubles and promises them that, He will appear in the world to destroy the demons and save the devotees.

While Lord Kṛṣṇa is the Original Source of all incarnations, when these incarnations appear within the material world, They do so through Kṣīrodakaśāyī Viṣṇu.

5.11. PARAMĀTMĀ (SUPERSOUL)

Kṣīrodakaśāyī Viṣṇu is present by His expansion in the heart of every living being as Paramātmā or Supersoul and He directs their wanderings in the material world.

Kṛṣṇa says in *Bhagavad-gītā* (18.61 and 15.15)

īśvaraḥ sarva-bhūtānāṁ
hṛd-deśe 'rjuna tiṣṭhati
bhrāmayan sarva-bhūtāni
yantrārūḍhāni māyayā
(*Bhagavad-gītā* 18.61)

Translation: *"The Supreme Lord is situated in everyone's heart, O Arjuna, and is directing the wanderings of all living entities, who are seated as on a machine, made of material energy."*

sarvasya cāhaṁ hṛdi sanniviṣṭo
mattaḥ smṛtir jñānam apohanaṁ ca
vedaiś ca sarvair aham eva vedyo
vedānta-kṛd veda-vid eva cāham
(*Bhagavad-gītā* 15.15)

Translation: *"I am seated in everyone's heart, and from Me come remembrance, knowledge and forgetfulness. By all the Vedas, I am to be known. Indeed I am the compiler of Vedanta, and I am the knower of the Vedas."*

The Paramātmā form is also present in every atom of the universe. Brahmā declares in *Brahma-saṁhitā*:

eko 'py asau racayituṁ jagad-aṇḍa-koṭiṁ
yac-chaktir asti jagad-aṇḍa-cayā yad-antaḥ

aṇḍāntara-stha-paramāṇu-cayāntara-sthaṁ
govindam ādi-puruṣaṁ tam ahaṁ bhajāmi

(*Brahma-saṁhitā* 5.35)

Translation: *"He is an undifferentiated entity as there is no distinction between potency and the possessor thereof .In His work of creation of millions of worlds, His potency remains inseparable.* **All the universes exist in Him and He is present in His fullness in every one of the atoms that are scattered throughout the universe, at one and the same time. Such is the primeval Lord whom I adore."**

Thus, the Supreme Lord is all-pervading in a wonderful and inconceivable way, and He maintains every part of His creation.

5.12. THE DESTRUCTION OF THE UNIVERSE

When the time comes for the universe to be destroyed, Lord Śiva in his Rudra form performs the 'dance of destruction'.

When all the planets and living beings are destroyed, everything enters into Garbhodakaśāyī Viṣṇu.

Eventually all the universes move back into Mahā-Viṣṇu when He inhales, and all is quiet in the material energy till the time of the next creation. When Mahā-Viṣṇu breathes out again, the creation takes place once again. In this way the material world undergoes an eternal cycle of creation, sustenance and destruction.

5.13. THE MATERIAL WORLD IS LIKE A SPIDER'S WEB

SPIDER'S WEB	MĀYĀ-THE LORD'S ILLUSORY ENERGY
As the spider spins its web and after a while winds it back into itself;	Similarly the Supreme Lord creates this material world and after a while pulls it back within Himself.

As the spider's web traps many flies and other insects;	Similarly the illusory power (*māyā*) of the material energy traps and binds those spirit souls who are rebellious to God, and wish to enjoy independent of Him.
The insects in the web struggle hard to free themselves, only to discover that they have become more tightly bound.	Similarly, living entities in the material world struggle hard against the stringent laws of material nature to avoid misery and to gain happiness, only to find themselves immersed in greater suffering. The struggle for freedom becomes the very cause for great bondage.
Just as the flies in the web can only get free when someone from outside the web frees them;	Similarly, the living entities, which are bound in this material world by the shackles of *māyā*, can only be freed when someone who is already free, frees them.

Why is this so? Because the living entities are in ignorance, they do not know the nature of their bondage in the illusory energy and how to get free from it.

Before we talk of freedom, let us first discuss the nature of bondage. So, what is the nature of this bondage in the material world? And how does it work?

To know this we will have to understand the concept of the 'Three Modes of Material Nature' or 'The Three *Guṇas*'.

5.14. THE THREE MODES OF MATERIAL NATURE

Lord Kṛṣṇa says in the *Bhagavad-gītā* (14.5) that, *Prakṛti* or Material Nature is constituted of three qualities or *guṇas*:

- ***Sattva-guṇa*** **(the mode of goodness)**

- ***Rajo-guṇa*** **(the mode of passion)**
- ***Tamo-guṇa*** **(the mode of ignorance)**
- **These *guṇas* bind the living entity.**
- Everything in the material creation is characterized and influenced by these three modes.
- The modes are all pervading.
- **Consider the three primary colors: Red, Yellow and Blue.** By mixing blue and yellow, we get green, and by mixing red and blue, we get purple. By further mixing and over-mixing, all the wide varieties of colors in the world are created.
- **Similarly, the mixing and further intermixing of the three modes yields all the possible combinations to create the unlimited variety of species in this world.**

Everything in the material creation can be classified according to the three modes. Here is just a sample.

None of the three modes exist purely in the material world.

They are always mixed together in varying proportions.

	Sattva-guṇa (Mode of goodness)	*Rajo-guṇa* (Mode of passion)	*Tamo-guṇa* (Mode of ignorance)	Spiritual (Beyond three modes)
ANIMALS	Cow	Lion	Monkey	Human
TIME	Early morning	Day	Night	Any time for serving Kṛṣṇa

PLACE	Forest	City	Bar	Temple
FOOD	Fresh fruits, vegetables, grains	Spicy food	Meat, liquor	*Prasādam*
OBJECT OF WORSHIP	Demigods	Powerful men	Ghosts and spirits	Lord Kṛṣṇa

5.15. BONDAGE DUE TO THE THREE MODES

The word '*guṇa*' also means 'rope'.

The three modes are thus ropes that bind the conditioned soul to this material world.

Sattva-guṇa is like a rope of gold
Rajo-guṇa is like a rope of silver
Tamo-guṇa is like a rope of iron

If one is bound as a prisoner in a jail, does it matter if the ropes are made of gold, silver or iron? A prisoner is a prisoner, after all.

The nature of such bondage is described in *Bhagavad-gītā* (14.6-9):

- **"O sinless one, the mode of goodness being purer than the others, is illuminating, and it frees one from all sinful reaction. Those situated in that mode become conditioned by a sense of happiness and knowledge." (*Bhagavad-gītā* 14.6)**

- **"The mode of passion is born of unlimited desires and longings, O sun of Kuntī, and because of this the embodied living entity is bound to material fruitive actions." (*Bhagavad-gītā* 14.7)**

- **"O son of Bharata, know that the mode of darkness, born of ignorance, is the delusion of all embodied living entities. The results of this mode are madness, indolence and sleep, which bind the conditioned soul." (*Bhagavad-gītā* 14.8)**

- **"O son of Bharata, the mode of goodness conditions one to happiness; passion conditions one to fruitive action; and ignorance, covering one's knowledge, binds one to madness." (*Bhagavad-gītā* 14.9)**

All living beings are thus puppets in the hands of the nature of the three *guṇas*, but due to the influence of *māyā*, they think themselves independent.

They think they are the 'doers' whereas actually, it is the three modes that do everything. Lord Kṛṣṇa says in the *Bhagavad-gītā*:

prakṛteḥ kriyamāṇāni
guṇaiḥ karmāṇi sarvaśaḥ
ahaṅkāra-vimūḍhātmā
kartāham iti manyate
(*Bhagavad-gītā* 3.27)

Translation: "*The spirit soul bewildered by the influence of false ego thinks himself the doer of activities that are in actuality carried out by the three modes of material nature.*"

5.16. CHARACTERISTICS OF THE THREE MODES

We may thus summarize the characteristics of the three modes as follows:

	Sattva-guṇa	*Rajo-guṇa*	*Tamo-guṇa*
General characteristics	Purity, happiness, knowledge	Unlimited desires, hard work, greed, wordly pleasures	Foolishness, sleep, laziness, intoxication, uncleanliness
Result	Freedom from sinful reactions	Bondage to worldly activities and misery	Madness, foolishness
Next birth	Heavenly planets	Amongst wordly people on earth	Animal kingdom and hellish planets

5.17. KṚṢṆA IS BEYOND THE THREE MODES

Being the master of the three modes, Kṛṣṇa is forever transcendental to them .He can never come under their influence. Only those who are themselves under the influence of the three modes, think that Kṛṣṇa is under the influence of three modes. He says:

tribhir guṇa-mayair bhāvair
ebhiḥ sarvam idaṁ jagat
mohitaṁ nābhijānāti
mām ebhyaḥ param avyayam
(*Bhagavad-gītā* 7.13)

Translation: *"Deluded by the three modes (goodness, passion and ignorance), the whole world does not know Me, who am above the three modes and inexhaustible."*

mayādhyakṣeṇa prakṛtiḥ
sūyate sa-carācaram
hetunānena kaunteya
jagad viparivartate
(***Bhagavad-gītā*** **9.10**)

Translation: *"This material nature, which is one of My energies, is working under My direction, O son of Kuntī, producing all moving and non-moving beings. Under its rule this manifestation is created and annihilated again and again."*

5.18. REAL FREEDOM

Real freedom is to transcend the three modes, i.e. to 'break' the bondage of the three ropes.

This is practically impossible to do, because the modes are very powerful and insurmountable. But Lord Kṛṣṇa gives us the way out.

daivī hy eṣā guṇa-mayī
mama māyā duratyayā
mām eva ye prapadyante
māyām etāṁ taranti te
(*Bhagavad-gītā* 7.14)

Translation: *"This divine energy of Mine, consisting of the three modes of material nature, is difficult to overcome. But those who have surrendered unto Me can easily cross beyond it."*

Thus it is only by coming to the transcendental platform of devotional service to Lord Kṛṣṇa, can one experience real freedom and return to our original spiritual home, in the Vaikuṇṭha world.

5.19. TIME (KĀLA)

Time or *Kāla* is one of the five subjects discussed in the *Bhagavad-gītā.*

- **It is one of the energies of the Lord, hence it is also eternal.**

- In fact, Lord Kṛṣṇa declares: **"I am inexhaustible time".**
(*Bhagavad-gītā* 10.33)

- **Kṛṣṇa acts through the agency of time to control the world. Due to the *Kāla-śakti*, everything in the material world undergoes six phases of transformation, namely, creation, growth, maturity, production of by-product, decay and finally destruction.**

- Thus, time is the greatest subduer in this world and it ultimately destroys everything.

- As Lord Kṛṣṇa says in the *Bhagavad-gītā:* **"Time I am, the great destroyer of the worlds, and I have come here to destroy all people...." (*Bhagavad-gītā* 11.32)**

- **The living entity performs activities in this world induced by *Prakṛti*, with the sanction of the Lord and under the control of Time.**
- Time moves unidirectionally in the material world and creates division of past, present and future.
- Time manifests also as various divisions in the cycle of creation, sustenance and destruction of the universe.
- **Since time is energy of the Lord, it must be used only in the Lord's service.**
- In other words, we should never waste time; rather we should try to spend as much as possible to serve Kṛṣṇa.

5.20. DIVISION OF TIME

The Vedic scriptures give detailed descriptions of time-scales, from the micro-level within the atom, to the macro level of the entire material creation.

Given below is some fascinating information on the divisions of time.

MICRO TIME SCALES		
One truṭi	8 / 13,500	second
One vedha	8 / 135	second
One lava	8 / 45	second
One nimeṣa	8 / 15	second
One kṣaṇa	8 / 5	seconds

One kāṣṭhā	8	seconds
One laghu	2	minutes
One daṇḍa	30	minutes
One prahara	3	hours
One day	12	hours
One night	12	hours
One pakṣa	15	days

Two **pakṣas** comprise one month and twelve months comprise one calendar year, or one full orbit of the sun.

A human being is expected to live up to one hundred years.

THE FOUR YUGAS	
Kali Yuga	= 4.32 lakh years
Dvāpara Yuga	= 8.64 lakh years (twice Kali-Yuga)
Tretā Yuga	= 12.96 lakh years (thrice Kali-Yuga)
Satya Yuga	= 17.28 lakh years (four times Kali-Yuga)
Catur Yuga or Divya Yuga	= 43.20 lakh years (ten times Kali-Yuga)

ONE FULL DAY OF BRAHMĀ

LIFETIME OF BRAHMĀ

1 full day	= 864 crore years
1 year of Brahmā (360 days)	= 864 x 360 crore years
Lifetime of Brahmā (100 years)	= 864 x 360 x 100 crore years
	= 31104000 crore years
	= 311.04 trillion years

DURATION OF THE UNIVERSE

Duration of the universe	= Lifetime of Brahmā
	= 1 Breath of Mahā-Viṣṇu
	= 311.04 trillion years

6.
DIFFERENT FORMS OF YOGA & THE TOPMOST YOGA SYSTEM

CRIFICE
RELIGION
MYSTIC YOGA
FRUITIV
VEDIC KNOWL

CHAPTER 6

DIFFERENT FORMS OF YOGA & THE TOPMOST YOGA SYSTEM

6.1. ONE MUST BECOME A YOGĪ

Lord Kṛṣṇa in the *Bhagavad-gītā* (6.46) declares that one must become a *Yogī*.

But, who is a '*Yogī*'? There are many misconceptions in this regard.

Let us first see what a *yogī* is not:

- **He is not one who merely performs physical exercises for good health.**
- **He is not simply one with matted locks of hair sitting in austere meditation in the Himalayas.**
- **He is not just a man with some extraordinary powers.**

6.2. WHAT IS 'YOGA'?

The world '*Yoga*' comes from the Sanskrit word '*yuj*' which means 'to reunite or link'. It is a link of love and service.

The Lord and the soul are eternally and constitutionally linked in a bond of love. To re-establish that link, is *yoga*.

- ***'Dharma'* means that which cannot be separated from something.**
- What is it that cannot be separated from fire? Heat and light.
- From sugar? Sweetness.

- Thus the '*dharma*' of fire and sugar are heat and sweetness respectively.
- **Similarly, the '*Dharma*' of the living being is to serve.**

We all have an innate tendency to love and serve. But presently that propensity is being directed towards the people and things of this world. Therefore, it simply ends in frustration.

- **Only when we repose our loving and serving propensity in the Supreme Lord, Śrī Kṛṣṇa, can we find real fulfillment and happiness.**
- **This is '*Sanātana-dharma*', or the eternal function of the soul.**

Having rebelled against the will of the Lord, we are now in the material world languishing in the miserable cycle of birth and death like the son of a rich man who leaves his father and ends up on the street as a beggar. The son can be happy only when he is re-united with his father.

Similarly, the soul can only be happy when it is brought back to the service of the Lord.

Thus, real '*yoga*' is the process of re-establishing the spirit soul in its eternal function, *Sanātana-dharma*', i.e. to love and serve God.

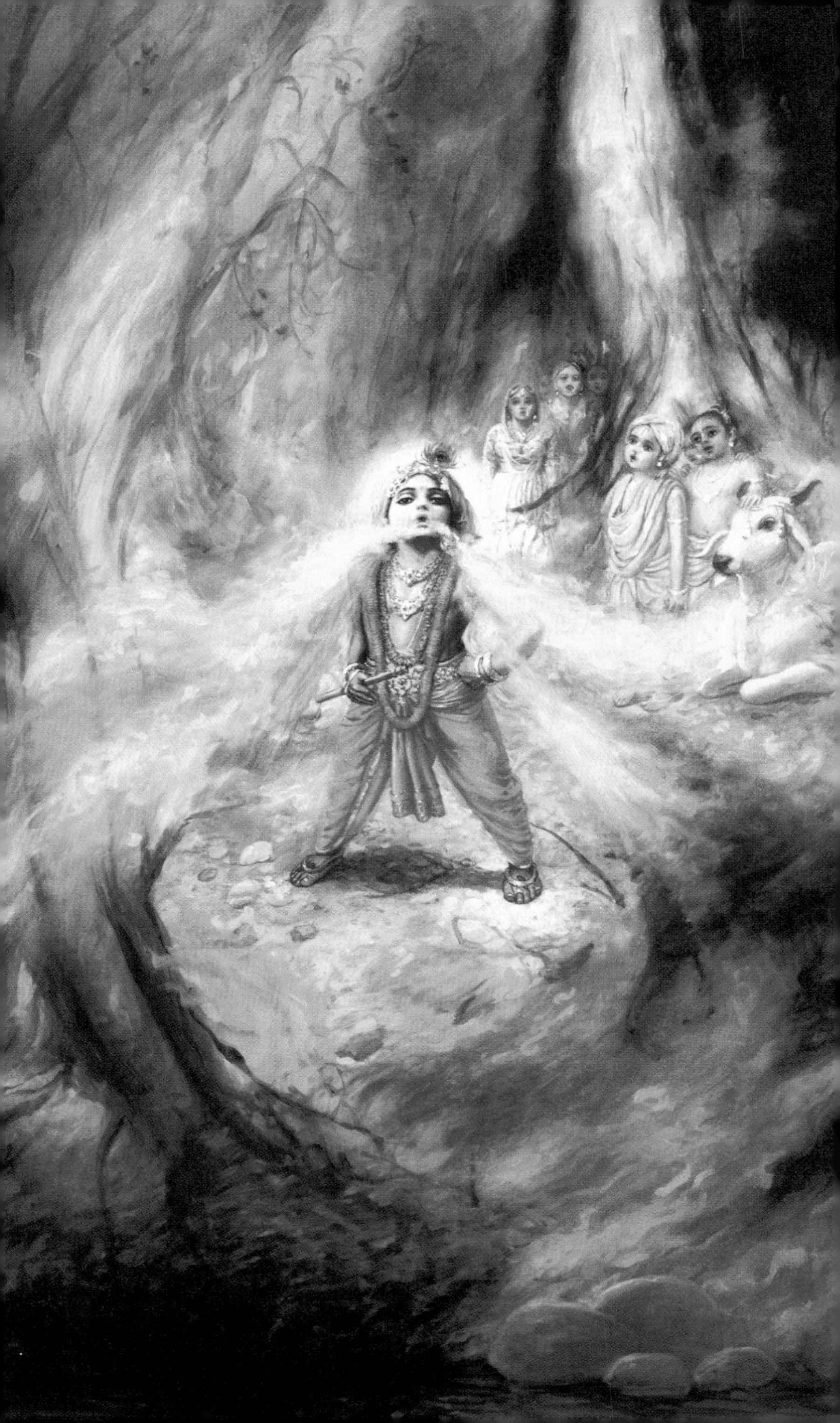

6.3. DIFFERENT CATEGORIES OF HUMAN BEINGS

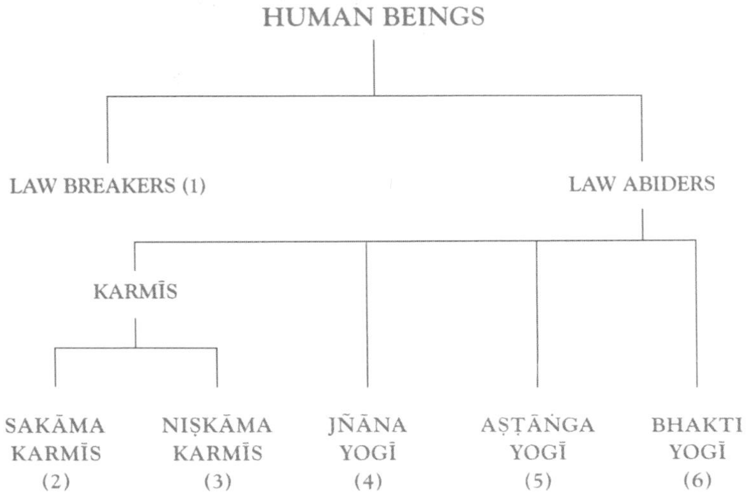

Thus we have six broad categories of human beings. Let us briefly discuss each of them.

Of these six, the first, the law breakers are considered two-legged animals.

The second, the *karma-kāṇḍīs*, are at least somewhat on the human platform.

And the other four are various types of *yogīs*.

6.4. THE LAW BREAKERS

They have no belief in God, rebirth or *karma*.

Their goal in life is to enjoy material sense gratification and they work hard for that.

They have no discrimination between piety and sin. They are only two- legged animals.

6.5. KARMA-KĀṆḌĪS

They are fruitive workers i.e. people who are eager to enjoy the fruits of their labor, but they are superior to the law-breakers because they regulate their sense enjoyment.

There is a certain section of the *Vedas* (the *karma-kāṇḍa* division) which prescribes various rituals for fulfillment of material desires through the worship of demigods.

Instead of acting whimsically and independently like the law-breakers do, the *karma-kāṇḍīs* at least accept the authority of the scripture and the demigods.

Thus they will gradually make progress in their understanding of the real purpose of life over a long period of time (may be many lives).

In the *Bhagavad-gītā*, Lord Kṛṣṇa calls such people 'unintelligent' because instead of trying to get free from the material world, they simply try to prolong their stay in it.

6.6. NIṢKĀMA KARMA YOGĪ

A *karma-kāṇḍī* may gradually come to realize the futility of material enjoyment because of its resultant suffering. At the same time, he knows that he cannot give up action, otherwise how could the body be maintained?

Thus he comes to the platform of becoming detached from the fruits of his action, following the principles enunciated in the famous *Bhagavad- gītā* verse:

karmaṇy evādhikāras te
mā phaleṣu kadācana

mā karma-phala-hetur bhūr
mā te saṅgo 'stv akarmaṇi

(*Bhagavad-gītā* 2.47)

Translation: *"You have a right to perform your prescribed duty, but you are not entitled to the fruits of action. Never consider yourself the cause of the results of your activities, and never be attached to not doing your duty."*

This is the first stage of *Niṣkāma karma yoga*. In the beginning, one may be detached by sacrificing the fruits of one's labor to some charitable cause like a hospital, social service etc. Although this is still material, at least by cultivating the practice of parting with the fruits of one's labor for a higher cause, one's mind is gradually purified. One begins to work without selfish desire for personal gain. Then one may be able to understand Kṛṣṇa Consciousness.

The *Niṣkāma karma yogī* has transcendence as his objective, even though he may or may not know that the Supreme Transcendence is Kṛṣṇa.

Lord Kṛṣṇa says, 'Work done as a sacrifice for Viṣṇu has to be performed; otherwise work causes bondage in this world.' This is the art of performing work without entanglement and is a higher stage of *karma yoga*.

Many people say "I'm a *Karma yogī*". Simply working very hard does not make one a *karma yogī*. One must at least be detached from the fruits of one's labor.

Lord Kṛṣṇa describes the qualities of *karma-yogī* in *Bhagavad-gītā*:

mayi sarvāṇi karmāṇi
sannyasyādhyātma-cetasā
nirāśīr nirmamo bhūtvā
yudhyasva vigata-jvaraḥ

(*Bhagavad-gītā* 3.30)

Translation: "*Therefore, O Arjuna, surrendering all your works unto*

Me, with full knowledge of Me, without desires for profit, with no claims to proprietorship, and free from lethargy, fight."

A *Karma yogī* must:

- **offer fruits of labor to God**
- **work in spiritual consciousness**
- **be detached from the fruits of labor**
- **give up the sense of proprietorship**
- **work without laziness**

Gradually, the *karma yogī* seeks higher understanding of something beyond this world.

6.7. JÑĀNA YOGĪS

When one tries to find the Absolute Truth, which is beyond this material world, by the process of negation ("*neti, neti*" i.e. "not this, not this"), he is called a *jñāna yogī.*

Jñāna yoga is the process of trying to understand the Absolute Truth through the cultivation of philosophical knowledge.

The *jñāna yogī* understands the Absolute Truth as the impersonal Brahman, the formless and eternal spiritual reality beyond this temporary material world.

They may wish to merge their spiritual identity into the impersonal Brahman. They perform severe austerities and also try to understand the Truth by philosophical speculation and word jugglery.

Lord Kṛṣṇa explains in the *Bhagavad-gītā* that, this path is ridden with great trouble and difficulty.

kleśo 'dhika-taras teṣām
avyaktāsakta-cetasām

avyaktā hi gatir duḥkhaṁ
dehavadbhir avāpyate
(*Bhagavad-gītā* 12.5)

Translation: *"For those whose minds are attached to the unmanifested, impersonal feature of the supreme, advancement is very troublesome. To make progress in that discipline is always difficult for those who are embodied."*

6.8. AṢṬĀṄGA YOGĪS

It is a meditative process to control the mind and the senses and to ultimately focus one's concentration on the Supreme.

It is an eight fold process consisting of: *yama, niyama, āsana, prāṇāyāma, pratyāhāra, dhāraṇā, dhyāna and samādhi.*

By initially following strict codes of conduct, and then practicing some physical and breathing exercises, one tries to meditate on the Paramātmā, the Lord in the heart. Whenever the unwanted, disturbing thoughts come one drives them away. As one advances in the meditation process, then finally one is able to achieve full absorption in the Lord. It is a very rigorous, strict and difficult regime and discipline to follow.

Aṣṭāṅga yogīs lift the soul up and eventually the soul may depart at a time of their choice through the '*brahma-randhra*', which is a tiny hole in the top of the skull. Then the perfected *yogī* may go to any destination in the universe.

In certain variations of this *yoga*, *sādhakas* try to activate the '*kuṇḍalinī*' - certain subtle psycho-physical energies stored in the body. This is however, very dangerous and even for those who succeed, they lose sight of the ultimate goal of life.

Often, strict practice of *aṣṭāṅga yoga* awards the *yogī* certain extraordinary

powers, which are simply material by-products of the process. Some of these powers (called '*siddhis*'): *aṇimā, laghimā, prāpti, īśitva, prākāmya, vaśitva and kāmāvasāyitā* i.e. becoming lighter than the lightest, heavier than heaviest, obtaining anything of one's choice, controlling others and so on.

Even genuine *aṣṭāṅga yogīs* look at these *siddhis* with contempt as they are simply distractions on the path.

Devotees of the Lord, in particular, are not at all impressed by a display of such powers, because they understand these things to be material, insignificant and irrelevant. The substance of life is devotion to God nothing else.

When Lord Kṛṣṇa described the process of *aṣṭāṅga yoga* to Arjuna in the 6th Chapter of *Bhagavad-gītā*, with all its strict requirements (e.g. celibacy, freedom from ego, fear and material desires, going to a secluded place, controlling the mind etc.), Arjuna said it was very difficult for him to follow.

How then can this process be applicable for us ordinary people of Kali Yuga? Therefore, *aṣṭāṅga yoga* is not practical for this age.

Some *aṣṭāṅga yogīs* prefer to worship the impersonal Brahman and others develop attachment for the Lord in the heart.

Gradually, the *aṣṭāṅga yogī* may advance to the point of beginning to render devotional service to the Supreme Lord. He has now arrived at the platform of *Bhakti Yoga*.

6.9. BHAKTI YOGA

***Bhakti yoga* is the *yoga* of selfless, ecstatic love of God by rendering devotional service.**

It involves engaging all one's senses in the service of the Supreme Lord, who is the master of the senses.

It makes us transcend all material designations, purifies the heart and senses and arouses love of God within.

Prahlāda has defined '*Bhakti*' or devotional service to the Lord as a nine- fold process. One can attain perfection in *Bhakti yoga* by adopting any one of these processes.

śrī-prahrāda uvāca

śravaṇaṁ kīrtanaṁ viṣṇoḥ
smaraṇaṁ pāda-sevanam
arcanaṁ vandanaṁ dāsyaṁ
sakhyam ātma-nivedanam
iti puṁsārpitā viṣṇau
bhaktiś cen nava-lakṣaṇā
kriyeta bhagavaty addhā
tan manye 'dhītam uttamam
(*Śrīmad-Bhāgavatam* 7.5.23-24)

Translation: *Prahlāda Mahārāja said: "Hearing and chanting about the transcendental holy name, form, qualities, paraphernalia and pastimes of Lord Viṣṇu, remembering them, serving the lotus feet of the Lord, offering the Lord respectful worship with sixteen types of paraphernalia, offering prayers to the Lord, becoming His servant, considering the Lord one's best friend, and surrendering everything unto Him (in other words, serving Him with the body, mind and words) — these nine processes are accepted as pure devotional service. One who has dedicated his life to the service of Kṛṣṇa through these nine methods should be understood to be the most learned person, for he has acquired complete knowledge."*

The chart below lists the nine process and also examples of great devotees who perfected their life by adopting them:

Process	Meaning	Names of devotees who attained perfection through this process
Śravaṇaṁ	Hearing about the Lord	Parīkṣit Mahārāja
Kīrtanaṁ	Speaking/ singing about the Lord	Śukadeva Gosvāmī
Smaraṇaṁ	Remembering the Lord	Prahlāda Mahārāja
Arcanaṁ	Worshipping the Deity of the Lord	Pṛthu Mahārāja
Vandanaṁ	Offering prayers to the Lord	Akrūra
Pāda-sevanam	Serving the Lord's lotus feet	Lakṣmī - devī
Dāsyaṁ	Acting as the Lord's servant	Hanumān
Sakhyam	Being friends with the Lord	Arjuna
Ātma-nivedanam	Surrendering everything to the Lord	Bali Mahārāja

The great devotee Ambarīṣa Mahārāja perfected his life by adopting all the nine processes of devotional service.

Bhakti yoga is the easiest, quickest and most effective *yoga* process to achieve the perfection of life.

PARĪKṢIT MAHĀRĀJA

ŚUKADEVA GOSVĀMĪ

PRAHLĀDA MAHĀRĀJA

PṚTHU MAHĀRĀJA

AKRŪRA

LAKṢMĪ - DEVĪ

HANUMĀN

ARJUNA

BALI MAHĀRĀJA

AMBARĪṢA MAHĀRĀJA

6.10. THE YOGA LADDER

The path leading up to God is like a ladder, the *yoga* ladder. The different yogic processes are like rungs on the ladder. ***Bhakti Yoga*** **is like the topmost rung. In fact, *Bhakti Yoga* is like an elevator or lift, that takes us very easily and quickly to the top.** Trying to reach the top through the other processes means that we have to climb the stairs all the way to the top. This is naturally very slow and cumbersome.

In other words, the normal long-route would be for one to evolve gradually over many life times through all the six stages i.e. the kinds of human beings that have been discussed earlier, namely, law-breakers, *karma-kāṇḍīs*, *karma- yogīs*, *jñāna yogīs*, *aṣṭāṅga yogīs* and finally *bhakti yogīs*.

So one should save time, energy and inconvenience, and adopt the risk-free process of *Bhakti Yoga* immediately. The *yoga* ladder is shown below:

BHAKTI (LOVE OF GOD)

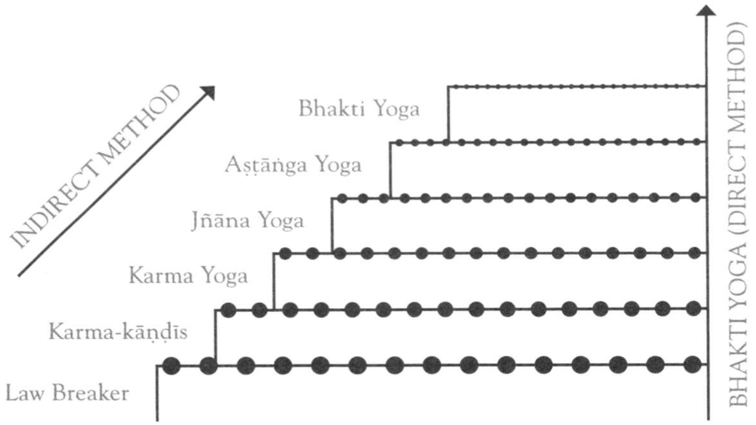

Bhakti yoga is independent, but all other *yogas* are dependent on it for achieving ultimate perfection.

In other words, *Bhakti yoga* is sufficient in itself to achieve perfection, but, along with the other processes, *Bhakti yoga* is required for perfection.

At any stage of the **yoga** ladder, one may take to ***Bhakti yoga***. The horizontal dotted lines in the above diagram show this.

What is it that is required for one to come to *Bhakti yoga* from any stage of the *Yoga* ladder?

- **The answer is: the association of devotees.**

Given below are examples of how other *yogīs* became *bhaktas* or devotees simply by association with the Lord or His devotees.

6.11. COMING TO BHAKTI YOGA

LAW BREAKERS: THE SINFUL HUNTER MṚGĀRI WAS CONVERTED INTO A KIND, COMPASSIONATE DEVOTEE BY ASSOCIATION OF THE GREAT NĀRADA MUNI. NĀRADA MUNI ALSO TRANSFORMED A SINFUL DACOIT INTO A SAINT, WHO THEN BECOME KNOWN AS VĀLMĪKI.

KARMA KĀṆḌĪ: KING PRĀCĪNABARHIṢAT WAS COMPLETELY IMMERSED IN KARMA KĀṆḌA BUT BY THE MERCY OF NĀRADA MUNI HE BECAME A DEVOTEE.

JÑĀNA YOGĪ: THE FOUR KUMĀRAS WERE IMPERSONALISTS, BUT BY SMELLING THE FRAGRANCE OF THE TULASĪ LEAVES OFFERED TO THE LOTUS FEET OF THE LORD, THEY BECAME DEVOTEES.

AṢṬĀṄGA YOGA: BY COMING IN CONTACT WITH AMBARĪṢA MAHĀRĀJA, THE POWERFUL MYSTIC YOGĪ DURVĀSĀ MUNI DEVELOPED THE UNDERSTANDING OF THE GREATNESS OF DEVOTEES.

6.12. BHAKTI YOGA - THE TOPMOST YOGA SYSTEM

Thus, the *Bhakti yogī* is the topmost *yogī* and this is clearly declared by Lord Kṛṣṇa in *Bhagavad-gītā*:

yoginām api sarveṣāṁ
mad-gatenāntar-ātmanā
śraddhāvān bhajate yo māṁ
sa me yukta-tamo mataḥ
(*Bhagavad-gītā* 6.47)

Translation: "*And of all yogīs, the one with great faith who always abides in Me, thinks of Me within himself, and renders transcendental loving service to Me—he is the most intimately united with Me in yoga and is the highest of all. That is My opinion.*"

There is a misconception that *Bhakti yoga* is for sentimentalists and *jñāna yoga* is for those who are intelligent and seeking knowledge.

Actually, one can come to *Bhakti* only after cultivating many lifetimes of knowledge, as confirmed by Lord Kṛṣṇa (*Bhagavad-gītā* 7.19).
In other words, *Bhakti* is the culmination and the very purpose of acquiring *jñāna*.

bahūnāṁ janmanām ante
jñānavān māṁ prapadyate
vāsudevaḥ sarvam iti
sa mahātmā su-durlabhaḥ
(*Bhagavad-gītā* 7.19)

Translation: "*After many births and deaths, he who is actually in knowledge surrenders unto Me, knowing Me to be the cause of all causes and all that is. Such a great soul is very rare.*"

Furthermore, one who has taken to devotional service must be understood to have already performed all other processes of *yoga* in previous lives.

Therefore, only the most intelligent persons take to the devotional service of the Lord.

6.13. THE DEVOTEES ARE DESTINED FOR THE SPIRITUAL WORLD

Those who become *Bhakti yogīs* have a very bright and happy future.

They are meant to go to Kingdom of God to engage in eternal, blissful and loving pastimes with the Supreme Lord.

This is the ultimate destination and perfection of life. There is nothing higher to be achieved. This is the goal of *yoga*.

6.14. THE DIFFERENT RASAS

In the spiritual world, one may love and serve the Lord in various '*Rasas*' or mellows – in neutrality, as His servant, as His friend, as His parent and as His lover.

These relationships and dealings are purely spiritual and have nothing to do with similar relationships of the material world.

As far as we are concerned, we may simply serve the Lord in the mood of a servant. He is our Lord and master and we are His eternal servants.

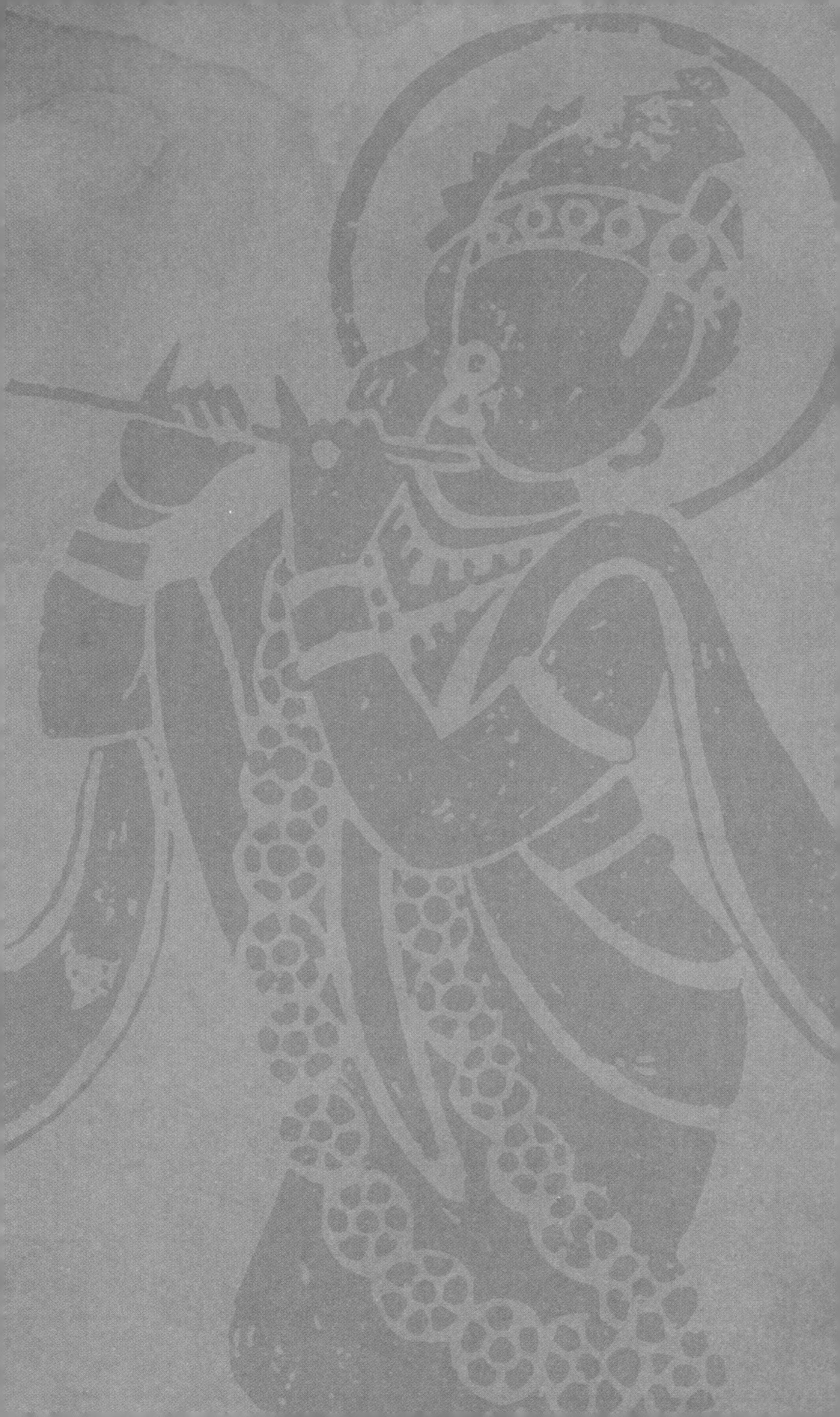

7. PRACTICAL APPLICATION OF BHAGAVAD-GĪTĀ

50

CHAPTER 7

PRACTICAL APPLICATION OF BHAGAVAD-GĪTĀ

7.1. JÑĀNA AND VIJÑĀNA

Theoretical knowledge (*jñāna*) becomes realized knowledge (*vijñāna*) when it is put into practice.

Bhagavad-gītā was spoken, not to a *sannyāsi*, or in an *āśrama* in the Himalayas, but to Arjuna, a householder and a warrior, and on the battlefield.

This means that the divine message of Lord Kṛṣṇa is meant for all of us, whether we are young or old, householders, or renounced.

7.2. THE 'DO'S' AND 'DON'TS'

Why are there so many rules and regulations in spiritual life?

The answer is simple. A doctor imposes many 'do's' and 'don'ts' upon his patients to facilitate the patient's recovery to normal health.

If the patient follows these restrictions properly, he will recover quickly, otherwise the illness will prolong.

Similarly, everyone in this material world is spiritually 'sick' and needs urgent 'treatment'. This treatment too, therefore, like medical treatment, has several do's and don'ts which are ultimately beneficial for spiritual 'recovery'.

One who voluntarily and sincerely submits to such a discipline will make quick spiritual advancement.

When Arjuna says to Lord Kṛṣṇa in the *Bhagavad-gītā* (6.34) that, controlling the mind is extremely difficult, Lord Kṛṣṇa agrees but declares that it is possible by '*abhyāsa*' (constant practice) and '*vairāgya*' (renunciation). (*Bhagavad-gītā* 6.35)

cañcalaṁ hi manaḥ kṛṣṇa
pramāthi balavad dṛḍham
tasyāhaṁ nigrahaṁ manye
vāyor iva su-duṣkaram
(*Bhagavad-gītā* 6.34)

Translation: *"For the mind is restless, turbulent, obstinate and very strong, O Kṛṣṇa, and to subdue it, I think, is more difficult than controlling the wind."*

śrī-bhagavān uvāca

asaṁśayaṁ mahā-bāho
mano durnigrahaṁ calam
abhyāsena tu kaunteya
vairāgyeṇa ca gṛhyate
(*Bhagavad-gītā* 6.35)

Translation: *"Lord Śrī Kṛṣṇa said: O mighty-armed son of Kuntī, it is undoubtedly very difficult to curb the restless mind, but it is possible by suitable practice and by detachment."*

We can understand '*abhyāsa*' to mean, acceptance of many do's in spiritual life and '*vairāgya*' to mean, acceptance of many don'ts.

The do's help us advance on the spiritual path, while following the dont's prevents us from falling back into materialistic consciousness.

Some of these important do's and don'ts are enumerated below.

7.3. ASSOCIATION OF DEVOTEES

The most important step we can take in life is to enter into in the company of devotees of Lord Kṛṣṇa as much as we can.

A devotee is very rarely found. The *Śrīmad-Bhāgavatam* explains that amongst millions of various *yogīs* and perfected beings, hardly one is a devotee of the Lord.

Even a moment's association with the devotees of the Lord is more valuable than even liberation and elevation to heavenly planets, what then to speak of ordinary material benedictions. So says the *Śrīmad-Bhāgavatam*.

Even by just a moment's association with devotees of the Lord, the door to the path of perfection is opened.

Therefore, never considering devotees to be ordinary and never seeing them from a mundane point of view (i.e. as being poor or rich, belonging to this caste or community or that, educated or uneducated etc), one should try to associate with them in a humble and devotional spirit.

One can obtain something only from where it is available. *Bhakti* is available only in the association of devotees, nowhere else. Thus says the Supreme Lord Himself again and again.

7.4. MAKING FRIENDS WITH DEVOTEES

Having come into the association of devotees, one should make friends with them and try to develop pure, spiritual relationships with them.

"Man is a social animal", so the saying goes. One needs friends and well - wishers for company.

Instead of befriending and associating with those who have no interest in spiritual life, one should rather spend more time with devotees.

In such association one gains encouragement, inspiration and spiritual strength to withstand the strong worldly current of *māyā*, which at every moment tries to push one back from devotional service.

7.5. HEARING DISCOURSES

In the association of devotees, the subject of conversation should be *Kṛṣṇa-kathā,* i.e. subjects dealing with the Lord, His devotees and *Bhakti*. Lord Kṛṣṇa explains in *Bhagavad-gītā* that, devotees take pleasure only in this.

mac-cittā mad-gata-prāṇā
bodhayantaḥ parasparam
kathayantaś ca māṁ
nityaṁ tuṣyanti ca ramanti ca
(*Bhagavad-gītā* 10.9)

Translation: *"The thoughts of My pure devotees dwell in Me, their lives are fully devoted to My service, and they derive great satisfaction and bliss from always enlightening one another and conversing about Me."*

The process of hearing is very powerful and important.

Divine messages and vibrations like the *Bhagavad-gītā* or the Holy Name penetrate into the heart through the ear and arouse love of God.

Whatever be our social or economic position, this should be our main activity.

Particularly in Kali-yuga '*śravaṇaṁ*' and '*kīrtanaṁ*' are most important.

7.6. SAṄKĪRTANA

'*Saṅkīrtana*' means the congregational chanting of the Holy Names

of the Lord. This is perfect (or '*samyak*') *kīrtana* recommended for this age. Every age has its own recommended *yuga-dharma*.

SATYA-YUGA

TRETĀ-YUGA

DVĀPARA-YUGA

KALI-YUGA

- For Satya -yuga it was Meditation
- For Tretā-yuga Sacrifice
- For Dvāpara-yuga Temple Worship and
- For Kali-yuga *Saṅkīrtana*

kṛte yad dhyāyato viṣṇuṁ
tretāyāṁ yajato makhaiḥ
dvāpare paricaryāyāṁ
kalau tad dhari-kīrtanāt
(*Śrīmad-Bhāgavatam* 12.3.52)

Translation: *"Whatever result was obtained in Satya-yuga by meditating on Viṣṇu, in Tretā-yuga by performing sacrifices, and in Dvāpara-yuga by serving the Lord's lotus feet can be obtained in Kali-yuga simply by chanting the Hare Kṛṣṇa mahā-mantra."*

The scriptures say that, "there is no other way, no other way, no other way….."

harer nāma harer nāma
harer nāmaiva kevalam
kalau nāsty eva nāsty eva
nāsty eva gatir anyathā
(*Bṛhan-nāradīya Purāṇa* 38.126)

Translation: *"In this age of quarrel and hypocrisy the only means of deliverance is chanting the holy name of the Lord Hari. There is no other way. There is no other way. There is no other way."*

Lord Caitanya Mahāprabhu is the same Lord Kṛṣṇa Himself who advented five hundred years ago to propagate the chanting of the Holy Names and to inaugurate the *yuga- dharma* for Kali yuga.

He has instructed the world to chant the *Mahā-mantra* that is recommended in the *Kali-santaraṇa Upaniṣad:*

Hare Kṛṣṇa, Hare Kṛṣṇa, Kṛṣṇa Kṛṣṇa, Hare Hare
Hare Rāma, Hare Rāma, Rāma Rāma, Hare Hare

This is the great, easy, effective and most sublime method of deliverance from the darkness of this material world.

It can purify the heart and produce pure love of God, *Bhakti.*

Therefore, one should try to participate in such *Saṅkīrtana* as much as possible.

7.7. JAPA

The holy name should also be chanted individually on one's chanting beads.

This is a very important and beneficial discipline as it helps us to gradually awaken love of God.

Whilst there are no hard and fast rules for chanting the holy names, one should follow the guidelines recommended by the great *Ācāryas.*

Śrīla Prabhupāda, the Founder *Ācārya* of ISKCON, recommended that we chant at least 16 rounds of the Hare Kṛṣṇa *Mahā-mantra* on our beads.

- There are 108 beads in one 'mālā'. The holy names should be chanted aloud and very clearly and be heard attentively.
- The beads are necessary because they help us to concentrate on the holy name.
- Also, some authorities on 'Mudrā' believe that rolling the beads in between the fingers promote noble thoughts and calms the mind.

- Such regulated chanting also serves as a discipline and further more ensures that our mind does not fool us into thinking that we have chanted more than we actually have.

7.8. SEVĀ

'*Sevā*' means to render service to the Lord and His devotees. This is highly recommended in the scripture as a necessary requirement for the growth of our *Bhakti*.

It helps to bring about purity, humility, joy, togetherness and community spirit when it is done in the right mood and right manner, for the right purpose.

Doing *sevā* is actually an honor, a great privilege and a good fortune,

so one should never take '*sevā*' lightly or for granted. To be given the opportunity to serve the Greatest Personality of creation is not a small thing.

Example of '*sevā*' are: cooking for the Deities, preparing garlands or jewellery for Them, cleaning the Temple, helping in publication or preaching work, donating to the Temple, and so on.

Ambarīṣa Mahārāja was a great King and devotee. He has set the example of how one must be willing to do even the most menial service, however big one may be in the world.

7.9. DEITY WORSHIP

The Deity or '*mūrti*' in the Temple is directly the Supreme Lord. There is no difference. Lord Kṛṣṇa has a pure, spiritual form.

We need spiritual eyes to see Him. But very kindly He has made Himself available within material elements to accept our service and to give us His personal audience (*darśana*). So we should never see the Deity as a piece of stone or wood. **He is directly the Supreme Lord Himself.**

There is a great deal of difference between a Deity and a statue or idol. A Deity is a bona fide representation of the Lord Himself, whereas an idol or statue is simply the figure of some other being like a human or a demigod.

The forms of the Deities are not made whimsically, but according to authorized descriptions in the scriptures and the realizations of great devotees of the Lord.

When we look at the Deities with faith and love, They reciprocate according to our level of faith. Otherwise, They will simply appear to the faithless eye to be 'idols'. We should try to take *darśana* of Their Lordships at least once every day. **We should dedicate all our activities to Them.**

7.10. PRASĀDAM

"You are what you eat", the saying goes. If we eat pure food we will become pure. If not, we will become contaminated.

In *Bhagavad-gītā* (3.13) Lord Kṛṣṇa says that, when one offers food to Him with love before eating, one becomes liberated from sin. **When food is not offered, it becomes a cause of sin.**

yajña-śiṣṭāśinaḥ santo
mucyante sarva-kilbiṣaiḥ
bhuñjate te tv aghaṁ pāpā
ye pacanty ātma-kāraṇāt
(*Bhagavad-gītā* 3.13)

Translation: "*The devotees of the Lord are released from all kinds of sins because they eat food which is offered first for sacrifice. Others, who prepare food for personal sense enjoyment, verily eat only sin*".

So we should offer whatever we wish to eat to the Lord in our house and eat nothing but that. And we can offer only what He accepts. He accepts only pure, *sāttvik* food (*Bhagavad-gītā* 9.26), so we cannot offer meat etc. to Him.

patraṁ puṣpaṁ phalaṁ toyaṁ
yo me bhaktyā prayacchati
tad ahaṁ bhakty-upahṛtam
aśnāmi prayatātmanaḥ
(*Bhagavad-gītā* 9.26)

Translation: *"If one offers Me with love and devotion a leaf, a flower, fruit or water, I will accept it."*

Prasādam is *karma*-free or sin-free food. And it is also very delicious.

7.11. READING SPIRITUAL LITERATURE

- Reading Spiritual Literature is highly recommended as it increases one's understanding, faith and conviction.
- It keeps one's mind and energies properly focused on the goal of life.
- Lord Kṛṣṇa explains that to study the *Bhagavad-gītā* is to worship Him with one's intelligence.
- Such reading must become a daily practice, even though sometimes it may become difficult.
- The fruits of such austerity, however, will be very sweet.

His Divine Grace A. C. Bhaktivedanta Swami Prabhupāda has provided for our benefit volumes and volumes of wonderful, enlightening and inspiring spiritual literature. One can nourish one's mind and intelligence by studying these books very diligently.

7.12. REGULARLY VISITING THE TEMPLE

To do all the above mentioned activities (e.g. hearing, chanting, association etc.) and to learn them, a proper place is required. That is a Temple of Lord Kṛṣṇa.

Temple is not simply a place where one visits occasionally to bow one's head, take *darśana* and perhaps make a donation. This is certainly good, but not enough.

So, what is the real purpose of visiting a Temple?

- The answer is: to be spiritually educated.
- A real Temple is a spiritual training centre, where we learn about Kṛṣṇa Consciousness and are given the proper atmosphere and inspiration to practice it.

Some people say "Why should we go to the Temple? God is everywhere."

- Certainly, God is everywhere, but do we have the eyes to see God everywhere?
- Real Temple is a place where we are trained to see God everywhere.
- And in any case, if God is 'everywhere', then is He not in the Temple too?

When people say "Show me God", we can take them to the Temple, show them the beautiful Deities of the Lord and teach them how to see and understand God.

7.13. MAKE YOUR HOME A TEMPLE

Sometimes people say: "I can practice *Bhakti* at home. What is the need to go to the Temple?"

Certainly one can, and should, practice *Bhakti* at home but in order to learn how to do that properly one must visit a bona fide Temple, where one can receive good guidance.

A child can study at home, yet the parents send him or her to school. Similarly, one should practice the principles of Kṛṣṇa Consciousness both at home and in the Temple, and indeed everywhere.

Hence by regularly visiting the Temple, one will learn how to make one's home a Temple; and eventually, how to make one's heart a Temple.

One should try to maintain an altar, i.e. a small Temple in the house. One may take guidance from devotees about how to do this.

Every day, family members should gather together at a suitable time to do *Hari-nāma-saṅkīrtana* and to read from a book like *Bhagavad-gītā*. Occasionally, devotees may be invited home for spiritual get-togethers.

Food should be first offered to the Deity/picture of Lord Kṛṣṇa in the house before anyone else eats.

Everything at home should be done for Him, considering Him to be the Lord and master of the house and the family.

In this way, one can keep Lord Kṛṣṇa in the centre of one's life and consciousness.

7.14. SPIRITUAL CHARITY

The scriptures say that householders must offer charity for the welfare of society and for the service of God.

There are different kinds of charity according to the Three Modes of Nature as described by Lord Kṛṣṇa in the *Bhagavad-gītā.*

Charity given for the sake of the Lord, for His service and to spread His message is the highest because it is transcendental, i.e. beyond the modes of nature.

Giving in charity protects the householders from greed and possessiveness.

By parting with the fruits of his labor for a higher cause, the householder is purified.

7.15. FASTING

Regulated fasting on specific occasions of spiritual significance is an important austerity for those seeking spiritual advancement.

In India, it is common to find people observing fasts on particular days of the week to appease certain demigods. This kind of fasting, however, has no spiritual value whatsoever.

Fasting should be done only on days or occasions connected with the Supreme Lord for His pleasure.

Devotees of Lord Kṛṣṇa generally fast on the following days :

Ekādaśī

This is the 11th day of the lunar fortnight and thus occurs twice a month. It is the "day of Lord Hari", a day on which Lord Kṛṣṇa is especially pleased to offer spiritual benedictions to those who perform austerities and devotional activities for His satisfaction.

Devotees try to maximize their hearing and chanting and other devotional activities on Ekādaśī. They also perform austerities like fasting.

Some devotees perform full fasting on this day, abstaining totally from food and water. This is called "Nirjala" fast.

However, it is sufficient to fast from grains and beans only, and partake of foodstuffs like fruits, vegetables, nuts, milk and so on.

Devotees should at least try to follow this standard.

Appearance days of the Lord and His *Avatāras*

The anniversaries of the descent of the Supreme Lord into this world in His different *avatāras* are celebrated joyously by devotees.

Festivals are held to glorify and remember the wonderful pastimes of the Lord. It is recommended that one fast on these auspicious days to invoke the pleasure of the Lord.

Fasting ("Nirjala") is prescribed till different times on each appearance day depending on what time of the day that particular *avatar* appeared.

Here is a sample:

DAY	APPEARANCE OF	FASTING TILL
Śrī Kṛṣṇa Janmāṣṭamī	Lord Kṛṣṇa	Midnight
Rāma-navamī	Lord Rāmacandra	Noon
Nṛsiṁha-caturdaśī	Lord Nṛsiṁha	Sunset
Gaura-pūrṇimā	Lord Caitanya Mahāprabhu	Moonrise

Appearance and Disappearance days of great *Ācāryas*

Just as the appearance days of the Lord's *avatāras* are important, so are the appearance and disappearance days of the Lords' great devotees.

The words 'birth' and 'death' are not used for such pure devotees of the Lord because they do not come into this world and leave the world like other ordinary people who are bound by their *karma*. Rather, these exalted personalities come as special messengers of the Lord to further His mission.

Fasting ("nirjala") till noon on specified appearance and disappearance days of the *Ācāryas* is recommended.

For specific dates and occasions it is advisable to keep a copy of the 'Vaiṣṇava Calendar", which is available at any ISKCON Temple. You may also consult devotees for further information.

7.16. PERSONAL HABITS

RISING EARLY

The early hours of the morning are in *sattva-guṇa*, the day-time in *rajo -guṇa* and night-time in *tamo-guṇa*.

The hours before sunrise and particularly the time ending about one and a half hours before sunrise, called *brāhma-muhūrta*, is very conducive for spiritual practice.

At this time, the atmosphere is clean and peaceful, the mind and body are fresh and rested. As the day progresses, however, many disturbances arise which do not permit one to focus one's mind and energies on worship, study of scripture and chanting.

Hence one should attempt to rise early every day to avail of the benefit that the *brāhma-muhūrta* offers.

One should not spend the early hours of the morning talking or working on petty or materialistic matters or in sleep.

This time should be reserved exclusively for one's spiritual development. In order to rise early one should go to bed early at night. Keeping late hours regularly is not a good practice for the spiritual aspirant.

KEEPING PHYSICALLY AND MENTALLY CLEAN

One keeps physically clean by taking bath at proper times and by avoiding contaminating activities, places, and people.

One should take bath immediately upon rising early, since sleep is in *tamo-guṇa* and its effect must be wiped out as soon as possible.

The contamination of sleep is not only physical but mental as well. Hence, the mind also needs to be purified immediately upon rising.

The mind is purified by chanting the holy names of the Lord. One should, therefore, make it a practice and habit to chant Lord Kṛṣṇa's names, not only as soon as one rises but at all other times too, whenever possible.

REGULATED LIFE

Lord Kṛṣṇa says in *Bhagavad-gītā* (6.17) that, one who wants to be a *yogī* must regulate his eating, sleeping, work and recreation.

yuktāhāra-vihārasya
yukta-ceṣṭasya karmasu
yukta-svapnāvabodhasya
yogo bhavati duḥkha-hā
(*Bhagavad-gītā* 6.17)

Translation: *"He who is regulated in his habits of eating, sleeping, recreation and work can mitigate all material pains by practicing the yoga system."*

Avoiding extremes, one should, therefore, lead a regulated and balanced life. One should eat at proper times, avoiding in - between snacks; one should eat wholesome, sāttvik food, avoiding commercial 'junk' foods', one should not over-eat. In conclusion, one should eat to live, rather than live to eat.

A daily quota of six and a half hours to seven hours of sleep is quite sufficient. Human life is very precious and one should not waste these valuable moments in excessive sleep.

One's working hours should also be regulated. The goal of life is not one's business, office, domestic chores or academic studies. While these things certainly have their place in life, they should not be the cause of the neglect of our spiritual life.

Therefore, one should manage one's time in such a way that one has enough time and energy left for spiritual activities like attending satsangs, chanting *japa*, reading Kṛṣṇa Conscious literature and so on.

In other words, one's spiritual needs are foremost and one's material life should be adjusted according to that and not vice-versa.

7.17. THE FOUR REGULATIVE PRINCIPLES

It is declared in the *Śrīmad-Bhāgavatam* that religion stands on four pillars: mercy, austerity, cleanliness and truthfulness.

There are four activities that directly violate these principles.

ACTIVITY	PRINCIPLE OF 'DHARMA' WHICH IS VIOLATED
Meat eating	Mercy
Intoxication	Austerity
Illicit sex	Cleanliness
Gambling	Truthfulness

These four activities are thus considered the pillars of sin.

They are the cause of great misery and must be scrupulously avoided by all, and particularly by those seeking spiritual advancement.

These 'Four Regulative Principles' are thus very important for the devotees of the Lord: No Meat-Eating, No Intoxication, No Illicit Sex and No Gambling.

7.18. NO MEAT-EATING

MEAT EATING IS CRUEL

Meat is a product of violence and cruelty and is thus against the principle of mercy.

Violence breeds violence. That is, meat–eaters are more prone to a violent mentality because they partake of products of violence.

Pythagoras has said that a person who sees nothing objectionable in the killing of animals gradually begins to think the same way about humans.

Civilized behavior is to survive with minimum possible pain to others. Meat-eating is thus a very uncivilized activity.

MAN MUST PROTECT ANIMALS

Lord Kṛṣṇa declares in the *Bhagavad-gītā* (14.4) that, He is the Father of all species of life. Thus, all living beings are brothers and sisters, part of one large family.

In a family, the elder or stronger children must protect the younger or weaker siblings.

But instead of protecting animals, man is killing them simply for the satisfaction of his tongue. This is therefore a very immoral and thoughtless act.

SEVERE KARMIC REACTIONS

Since killing animals is a great sin, humanity is suffering the terrible karmic consequences of such large-scale cruelty and violence.

Wars, terrorism, ghastly crimes etc, are all evidence of how humans are being slaughtered themselves as a reaction to terrible sins like animal-killing particularly the killing of Mother Cow.

By the Law of *Karma*, killers of animals are destined to take animal forms in future lives and be slaughtered themselves.

The *Manu-saṁhitā* says that, six parties are implicated in the sin of animal killing: the one who gives permission to kill, the killer, the helper, the purchaser, the cook and the one who eats the meat.

MEAT IS A DEAD BODY

The famous British author George Bernard Shaw declared that, he was a vegetarian because he did not wish to make his stomach a graveyard.

When the meat arrives at one's dining table in nice cutlery, one forgets the harsh reality that one is about eat a dead body, because it is so well presented.

Meat is simply rotten flesh that is somehow preserved by use of artificial means like refrigeration, spices and so on.

Meat is full of various toxins secreted internally by the animal in its fearful and agonizing dying moments.

Thus, meat being stale, unclean and violent in its origin, is *tamasic* food, food in the mode of ignorance.

MEAT IS NOT THE DESIGNATED FOOD FOR HUMANS

The way of Nature is '*Jīvo jīvasya jīvanam*' i.e. one species is food for another.

Every species has its designated food amongst other species. Meat is natural food for animals like the tiger, but not for human beings. The designated food for humans is vegetarian food.

The tiger does not come to eat our chapattis or rice, so why should we go to eat his food i.e. meat?

The human anatomy being very similar to that of a herbivore is specially suited for a vegetarian diet. The carnivore or meat-eating animal has specific anatomical features that are not found in herbivores and humans.

The chart below summarizes some of these points.

	CARNIVORE	HERBIVORE	HUMAN BEING
1	Has claws	No claws	No claws
2	Sharp, pointed front teeth to tear flesh	No sharp, pointed front teeth	No sharp, pointed front teeth
3	No pores on skin. Perspires through tongue to cool his body	Perspires through millions of pores on skin	Perspires through millions of pores on skin
4	Much stronger hydrochloric acid in stomach to digest tough animal muscle and bones	Stomach acid 20 times less strong than meat eaters	Stomach acid 20 times less strong than meat eaters
5	Intestinal tract relatively short so rapidly decaying meat can pass out of body	Intestinal tract relatively longer. Fruits and plants do not decay as rapidly, so can pass more slowly through body	Intestinal tract relatively longer

The above are only some of the reasons to avoid meat-eating.

The conclusion is that meat-eating (including fish and eggs) destroys spiritual consciousness and is thus to be avoided. The serious spiritual aspirant also gives up onion and garlic because these are also associated *tamasic* foods.

7.19. NO INTOXICATION

An intoxicated person is out of touch with reality and lives in a false world.

Living beings in this world are all already 'intoxicated' by the desire for sense gratification, in forgetfulness of Lord Kṛṣṇa. Artificial intoxicants, therefore, only serve to increase this forgetfulness further and take us towards hellish conditions of life.

Intoxicants make one incapable of performing any kind of austerity.

Liquor, drugs, tobacco products, 'pan' and 'pan masala,' 'gutkha' and even tea and coffee are intoxicants of various degrees and should be avoided.

7.20. NO ILLICIT SEX

This means no sex outside of marriage, and regulated sex even within marriage.

Illicit sex is against the principles of cleanliness – physical and mental.

Illicit sex makes one forget the goal of life and drags one down rogressively into lower modes of consciousness.

7.21. NO GAMBLING

Gambling destroys truthfulness. It creates greed and destroys peace of mind, and ultimately ruins everything.

Apart from the obvious meaning of the word; 'gambling' also includes such activities as speculation on the stock market and high risk business ventures.

Also included are such apparently innocent amusements as lottery tickets and games like horse racing and TV shows like, "Kaun Banega Crorepati?" etc.

Gambling makes one lazy and greedy because it creates a spirit of wanting something for nothing, without honest work input. Devotees of the Lord, therefore, avoid all types of gambling activities.

7.22. AVOID ASSOCIATION OF NON-DEVOTEES

This is one of the very important 'don'ts' in spiritual life. In as much as it is important to obtain association of devotees, it is as important to avoid association of non-devotees.

Such bad association is not only a troublesome distraction and waste of time, but is also the root of evil and downfall.

Association with non-devotees may be, however, unavoidable for professional or social reasons. In such cases, one should keep it to the minimum required for the sake of professional or social courtesy.

One should not associate with non-devotees to take pleasure in the things they take pleasure in. (Remember the story of the Monkey and the Crocodile. Associate with non-devotees when necessary, but don't give your heart to them).

7.23. AVOID MUNDANE TV / CINEMA

The mass media, headed by TV and cinema, has effectively done in a few decades what many centuries of history could not do: it has destroyed spiritual culture and introduced in a very powerful way the modern materialistic culture of greed, enjoyment and power.

TV kills all good qualities, no wonder it is called the "idiot box." Devotees should therefore seek their entertainment and enlightenment in association of devotees and in spiritual culture (i.e. devotional music, drama, literature and so on).

7.24. CONCLUSION

Always think of Lord Kṛṣṇa. Never forget Lord Kṛṣṇa.

This is the sum and substance, and the very purpose, of all rules and regulations.

Every moment of human life is precious. Once gone, it cannot be purchased even for crores of rupees. Therefore, one should use it for the purpose for which it has been given to us, namely, to develop our Kṛṣṇa Consciousness.

Thus, following the dictum "Simple Living, High Thinking", we can make our human life perfect.

8.
SANSKRIT PRONUNCIATION & DIACRITIC GUIDE

CHAPTER 8

SANSKRIT PRONUNCIATION & DIACRITIC GUIDE

SANSKRIT PRONUNCIATION GUIDE

Throughout the centuries, the Sanskrit language has been written in a variety of alphabets. The mode of writing most widely used throughout India, however, is called *devanagari*, which means, literally, the writing used in "the cities of the demigods. " The *devanagari* alphabet consists of forty-eight characters : thirteen vowels and thirty-five consonants. Ancient Sanskrit grammarians arranged this alphabet according to practical linguistic principles, and this order has been accepted by all Western scholars. The system of transliteration used in this book conforms to a system that scholars have accepted to indicate the pronunciation of each Sanskrit sound.

The vowels are pronounced as follows:

SR.NO.		SR.NO.	
1.	**a** - as in b**u**t	7.	**ṛ** - as in **ri**m
2.	**ā** - as in f**a**r but held twice as long as **a**	8.	**ṝ** - as in **ree**d but held twice as long as **ṛ**
3.	**i**- as in p**i**n	9.	**i** - as in happ**i**ly
4.	**ī** - as in p**i**que but held twice as long as **i**	10.	**e** - as in th**ey**

5.	**u** - as in **pu**sh	11.	**ai** - as in **ai**sle
6.	**ū** - as in **ru**le but held twice as long as **u**	12.	**o** - as **go**
		13.	**au** - as **how**

The Consonants are pronounced as follows:

SR.NO.	GUTTURALS (pronounced from the throat)	SR.NO.	PALATALS (pronounced with the middle of tongue against the palate)
14.	**k** - as in **k**ite	19.	**c** - as in **ch**air
15.	**kh** - as in Ec**kh**art	20.	**ch** - as in staun**ch-h**eart
16.	**g** - as in **g**ive	21.	**j** - as in **j**oy
17.	**gh** - as in di**g-h**ard	22.	**jh** - as in he**dgeh**og
18.	**ṇ** - as in si**ng**	23.	**ñ** - as in ca**ny**on

SR.NO.	CEREBRALS (pronounced with the tip of tongue against the roof of the mouth)	SR.NO.	DENTALS (pronounced like cerebrals but with the tongue against the teeth)
24.	**ṭ** - as in **t**ub	29.	**t** - as in **t**ub
25.	**ṭh** - as in ligh**t-h**eart	30.	**th**- as in ligh**t-h**eart
26.	**ḍ** - as in **d**ove	31.	**d** - **d**ove

27.	**ḍh** - as in red-**h**ot	32.	**dh** - as in red-**h**ot
28.	**ṇ** - as in si**ng**	33.	**n** - as in **n**ut

SR.NO.	LABIALS (pronounced with lips)	SR.NO.	SEMIVOWELS
34.	**p** -**p**ine	39.	**y** -as in **y**es
35.	**ph** - as in u**p-h**ill	40.	**r** - as in **r**un
36.	**b** - as in **b**ird	41.	**l** - as in **l**ight
37.	**bh**- as in ru**b-h**ard	42.	**v** - as in **v**ine, except when preceded in the same syllable by the consonant, then as in s**w**an
38.	**m** - as in **m**other		

SR.NO.	SIBILANTS	SR.NO.	ASPIRATE
43.	**ś** - as in the German word *sprechen*	46.	**h** - as in **h**ome
44.	**ṣ** - as in **sh**ine		
45.	**s** - as in **s**un		

SR.NO.	ANUSVĀRA	SR.NO.	VISARGA
47.	**ṁ** - a resonant nasal sound as in the French word *bon*	48.	**ḥ** - a final **h**-sound; **aḥ** is pronounced like **aha**; **iḥ** like **ihi**.